651

F5
FLRe

SECRETARIAL AND ADMINISTRATION SPECIALIST UNITS

Carol Carysforth
Val Warrilow

NVQ LEVEL 2

D0314765

Heinemann Educational
a division of Heinemann Educational Books Ltd,
Halley Court, Jordan Hill, Oxford OX2 8EJ

OXFORD   LONDON   EDINBURGH
MADRID   ATHENS   BOLOGNA   PARIS
MELBOURNE   SYDNEY   AUCKLAND   SINGAPORE   TOKYO
IBADAN   NAIROBI   HARARE   GABORONE
PORTSMOUTH NH (USA)

© Carol Carysforth and Valerie Warrilow 1991

First published 1991

British Library Cataloguing in Publication Data
    Carysforth, Carol
    Business Administration: core units
    1. Business Practices
    I Title. II Warrilow, Valerie
    651

ISBN 0 435 450 02 6

Designed by Green Door, Basingstoke
Illustrated by Gecko, Bicester, Oxon
Printed in England
by Clays Ltd, St Ives plc

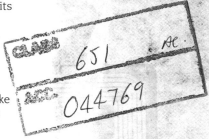

ACKNOWLEDGEMENTS

The authors would like to personally acknowledge the co-operation, assistance and support of friends and colleagues, whose combined expertise proved invaluable in the writing of these books.

Especial thanks for specialist help and advice are due to David Williams AIDPM, Peter Gold LIB, Duncan Isherwood RIBA, John Haworth FCA, Mavis Williams Cert Ed, AFTComm, Alex Clark and, not least, Margaret Berriman for her encouragement and guidance throughout.

The authors and publishers would also like to thank the following organisations for permission to reproduce copyright material:

The Automobile Association
Banking Information Service
Barclays Bank plc – Retailer Services
Barclays Bank plc – Banking Services
British Airways plc
British Gas plc
British Rail
British Telecom plc
Air France Holidays and French Travel Service
Guardian Royal Exchange Assurance
The Controller of Her Majesty's Stationery Office
Midland Bank plc
National Westminster Bank plc – Banking Services
National Westminster Bank plc – Retailer Card Services
The Post Office
Royal Bank of Scotland plc
French Railways SNCF
Safeguard Systems GB Ltd

CONTENTS

SECRETARIAL AND OFFICE ADMINISTRATION SPECIALIST UNITS

Telecommunications and data transmission

There is one, simple aim of telecommunications and data transmission systems:

- **to transmit information to people** *quickly* **and** *accurately no matter where they are.*

The system used will depend on whether the information is *verbal* or *written*, the distance involved, the time of day, where the person being called is likely to be and the equipment being used.

TELECOMMUNICATIONS SYSTEMS
Information can be transmitted

verbally:
- by telephone (to offices, cars, outside locations)
- via an answering machine
- to a pager or bleeper
- by a public address system or tannoy.

in writing:
- fax
- telex
- electronic mail (or Email – also called Elmail)
- communicating word processors and computers.

CHECK IT YOURSELF
Think about *why* an organisation may prefer to send certain types of information in written form, rather than verbally.

Try to list *five* occasions when it would be much better for the information to be written down.

The 'people' element
No matter which system is used, *people* are involved:

- passing on messages verbally
- writing down messsages
- using equipment.

Unless those involved – and this means you! – can carry out their part efficiently, then all the expensive technological equipment in the world is useless!

Section 1 – Telecommunications

TELEPHONE SYSTEMS

Organisations usually have one of two main types of telephone system installed:

- a PABX (private automatic branch exchange) (Fig. 1)   or
- a multiline or KTS (key telephone system) (Fig. 2).

Figure 1   **Figure 2**

PABX

A PABX is a switchboard, manned by an operator, which receives all incoming calls on behalf of the organisation. Calls are therefore handled *centrally* in one location. The switchboard may be in a separate room or operated by a receptionist/switchboard operator.

The largest PABXs today are digital, can support hundreds of extensions, and are programmed not only to offer a variety of facilities to extension users but also to undertake many functions automatically, eg transferring calls, bypassing busy extensions, even printing out updated telephone lists.

Multiline or KTS

With this telephone system all extensions in the organisation can receive incoming calls *or* one extension can be programmed to act as the switchboard. The maximum number of extensions is about 80, but most systems are smaller than this (more than about 25 means that an operator is required to route incoming calls).

Again a variety of facilities are available to extension users and the extensions are usually clearly labelled with a button per function. Some experts consider this means that users are more confident and capable of using all the facilities available than when ordinary extensions are installed. A good multiline system is upgradable to support a PABX if the business expands in the future.

Facilities on offer with PABX and multiline
The list below is not exhaustive but gives some idea of the facilities available on both systems. Not *all* the facilities mentioned can be found on *all* systems!

	PABX	Multiline
Queuing of incoming calls – so calls are answered in strict rotation	✓	✓
All extensions capable of making outgoing calls (PABX extension users usually have to dial 9 first)	✓	✓
Extensions can be barred from making certain calls if required (eg international calls)	✓	✓
Last number redial	✓	✓
Memory for frequently called numbers, accessible by extension users and abbreviated dialling	✓	✓
Conference calling (linking of two or more extensions plus outside call if required)	✓	✓
Light indicators on switchboard so that operator can see status of all calls/ extensions engaged	✓	✓

Feature		
LCD display on extensions to give call status, allow message displays, indicate which extension is calling	✗	✓
Diversions and hunting – extension users instruct system to follow them round the building when away from their office	✓	✓
Callback – if another extension is engaged, a number code dialled into the system instructs the phone to ring the caller and the other extension when it is free	✓	✓
Music on hold if required	✓	✓
Handfree answering (via loudspeaker)	✗	✓
On/off hook dialling ⸱	✗	✓
Call waiting tone to warn extension users another call is holding	✓	✓
Private circuit to enable branch offices to ring extensions direct	✓	✗
Call logging and costing – the system records all calls made, where to, duration and cost per extension	✓	✓
Automatic waiting return – calls not answered by an extension are automatically returned to the switchboard	✓	✗

CHECK IT YOURSELF

- What use do you think management might make of call logging, eg if they found one department was on the telephone for longer than anyone else, even though the same number of calls were made?
- Have you ever experienced 'music on hold'? What is your opinion of it – do you think customers prefer it – or detest it?

SPECIAL NOTE

A special PABX 'add on' feature is a computerised speech synthesiser (ie a computer 'voice') which says when a call is coming in and its status at any time at the touch of a button. It will also give prompts to the operator if required. This can be used to enable visually handicapped operators to operate the switchboard, as they may not be able to see the lights flashing.

Technology update

Some of the larger digital PABXs are linked to a VDU so that the operator can see the status of the whole system on screen at any time. They can also be networked (linked) to fax machines, word processors and computers, and voice and fax messages which come in overnight can be stored and retrieved.

System X

In many parts of the UK is it now possible for *home* telephone users to access some of the facilities listed earlier. This is because British Telecom has been busy converting telephone exchanges to a new digital system – known as System X. By the end of this century the system will be nationwide and will enable all users with a touchtone (multi-frequency (mf)) telephone to access any of the following Star Services for a small charge:

Reminder call	• automatically book your own alarm call
Charge advice	• so you are automatically informed how much a call has cost
Call diversion	• automatically transfer your calls to another number
Call waiting	• a signal will tell you another call is waiting *and* you can put the first on hold whilst you find out who it is
Three-way calling	• three people on different phones can be linked in the same conversation
Code calling	• to extend the memory of 'held' numbers and provide an abbreviated dialling facility
Call barring	• a message is automatically played to anyone who calls when you are away or out to say you are temporarily unavailable.

SPECIAL NOTE

- To use System X you need a multi-frequency (MF) telephone. You can identify you are on System X with these telephones because:
    - the system does not 'click' when you dial but produces an almost musical 'tone'
    - almost as soon as you finish dialling the other number starts to ring.
- MF telephones also have two special keys – found on most office extensions. A **star** (or **asterisk**) key and a **gate** (or **hash**) key. You need these keys to be able to use Star Services.
- The services *aren't* free! Get a booklet from British Telecom and find out the latest rates.

Star key   **Gate key**

Cell phones

You probably know these as car phones or mobile phones. There are three main types in use:

- mobile phones are fitted permanently in the car and run off the car battery
- hand portables can be carried around but are more expensive. The battery frequently needs recharging
- transportable phones are a cross between the two. They can be used in or out of a vehicle but have a rather bulky battery pack.

The system operates through base stations all over the UK each controlling a cell network with its own transmitter. A car travelling up the M1 or M6 would travel through several cell areas.

Calling someone on a car phone is easy – you just dial the car phone number. If the person has the phone switched off, or is travelling out of range, then a pre-recorded message tells you that the person you are calling is not available at present.

CHECK IT YOURSELF

Discuss with your tutor the reason for the growing popularity of these phones. What businesses do you think use them most and why?

THE SWITCHBOARD OPERATOR

A switchboard operator is the invisible receptionist for her organisation. She is judged on her voice, manner, speed and efficiency. Proper training and a good knowledge of the company are very important.

The switchboard operator must:

- answer calls promptly
- greet callers properly, eg 'Good Morning' and name of company
- operate the switchboard quickly and accurately
- give priority to incoming calls rather than to extension users
- direct incoming calls to the correct extensions
- if the extension is engaged give the caller the choice whether to hold or call back later
- keep callers who are 'holding' informed as to what is happening by regularly going back to them
- make outside calls if required and connect these to extensions
- use directories and other reference books quickly and accurately
- keep records such as fault reports and any other call logs that are required (eg international calls)
- quickly and easily identify which telephone service would be the most suitable at any given time
- be able to operate a wide variety of additional equipment – logging machines, answering machines, public address systems etc.

To fulfil these duties she must know:

- correct standard expressions ('Will you hold the line please?' *not* 'Hold on!')
- the telephone services available
- the organisation's functions, departments and personnel, plus who does what
- how to take messages quickly and accurately.

Reference books

The following reference books are likely to be needed by a
switchboard operator:

- local directory plus those for other areas called frequently
- Yellow Pages and Business Pages for the area
- call charge leaflets
- British Telecom Guide
- world atlas
- foreign phrase books (if appropriate) *or* useful phrase list for
  switchboard operators published by British Telecom.

TEST YOURSELF
As a switchboard operator you must not only know which books to use, but how
to look up numbers quickly and accurately.

How quickly can you find the following numbers:

1   Your local police station.
2   *Two* vets and *one* architect in the area.
3   A burglar alarm company (preferably a manufacturer).
4   *Any* local voluntary organisation.
5   Your nearest Customs & Excise office handling VAT enquiries.
6   Heathrow and Manchester airports.

Operator records

It is the operator's responsibility to maintain certain records, eg:

- a complete and up-to-date list of all extension numbers and
  users. It is usually better to list this in alphabetical order of
  people or offices *not* in numerical order of extensions. A
  laminated copy should be clearly visible near the
  switchboard.

- a list of all bleeper holders/numbers and priority codes (if used)
- a list of car phone numbers belonging to employees (eg representatives)
- an alphabetical list of organisations called frequently with their telephone numbers, plus names of contacts and extension numbers
- a fault book in which reported faults are recorded with date and time plus date and time of any follow up
- a log book for long distance or overseas calls if no logging equipment is installed
- a message pad – preferably one which allows duplicate copies to be made automatically.

Team work

In most organisations there will be a relief operator who will take over from the main operator for breaks, lunch-times etc. The hand-over is an important test of communication! The relief must be informed:

- of any calls outstanding
- of any important expected calls
- of any messages outstanding.

The updated information must, of course, be passed back to the main operator when that person returns.

Switchboard training

Some companies advertise for switchboard operators who are British Telecom trained. However, British Telecom will visit organisations where a new switchboard operator has been employed *or* if a new type of switchboard is installed the supplier will usually arrange training.

Operators also need help and co-operation from extension users who should:

- inform the switchboard if they will be away for any length of time
- inform the switchboard if they must not be disturbed *and* where calls can be redirected
- not ask the switchboard to get calls for them that they can easily make themselves

- give both the number they require *and* code if they are barred extension users
- be prepared to accept calls for their department and take a message if necessary – not expect the switchboard to do this for them
- *always* answer their extension correctly and pleasantly – even if interrupted whilst doing an important job.

! SPECIAL NOTE

Many reception and switchboard areas of large exporting companies have several clocks, clearly visible, showing the times in the different countries they deal with. These are placed alongside a clock showing the time in the UK.

These obviously help anyone who regularly makes international calls, as well as giving useful information to visitors to the organisation from abroad who may want to contact their own organisations.

TELEPHONE REFERENCE BOOKS

In addition to the ordinary telephone directory and Yellow Pages for their area, most businesses also keep:

- telephone directories for other areas they call regularly
- Business Pages (similar to Yellow Pages but with business suppliers, not retail outlets and services, and covers a wider area)
- an internal directory showing all extensions against departments or names of staff.

You should be able to use these easily to look up numbers you need both inside and outside your organisation.

⊞ CHECK IT YOURSELF

Look through your telephone directory and find out

- the difference between 071 and 081 when ringing London numbers
- the STD codes for Newport (Shropshire), Waterford (Southern Ireland), Castletown (Caithness), Preston (Dorset), Menai Bridge and Londonderry
- the International Direct Dialling (IDD) codes for Switzerland, Norway and Gibraltar
- the time difference between the UK and Burma
- the number of the speaking clock.

DIFFICULT CALLERS

Not all callers who contact an organisation will know who they want to speak to. Some may ask for confidential information, others may ask for something the switchboard operator has never heard of. Indeed there are a range of problem situations a switchboard operator must be able to cope with.

Below are given some of the most common types of difficult calls received. Generally a switchboard operator should never spend so long with one caller that other calls queue up behind. If you are busy then try to pass the call on to an extension as soon as possible.

The first time caller (who doesn't know who to speak to)

Listen carefully	**don't** assume you know what they want
Ask questions if necessary	**don't** put them through to the first person you think of
Suggest a name and tell them you are connecting them to that person	**don't** connect them without warning the extension user what the call is about and why you have referred it to them

The caller who wants confidential information

Make sure it is a confidential request, eg for personal information about staff	**don't** give out confidential information to anyone – if necessary say you don't know the answer
Find out who is calling	**don't** be 'easily impressed'
Transfer the call to an extension who **may** be able to help	**don't** forget to warn the extension who is calling – and what they want to know

The complaint/the angry caller

Listen sympathetically	**Don't** interrupt in the early stages of the conversation

Take down all the facts	**Don't** give vague excuses
Check you have these down correctly by reading them back to the caller	**Don't** put the blame on anyone
Explain to the caller you will pass on the problem to your supervisor immediately	**Don't** try to pretend the problem doesn't exist
Explain to the caller his/her complaint will be investigated	**Don't** make promises outside your control
Give a time when someone will call back	**Don't** delay in passing on the message to someone who can deal with it

The foreigner who speaks poor English/has a strong accent

Listen carefully	**Don't** speak quickly
Use simple English words	**Don't** use long sentences
Repeat carefully what you think is meant to check you are right	**Don't** shout!
Ask for help if you really cannot understand the caller at all	**Don't** become impatient

Nuisance callers (eg heavy breathing or worse!)

Stay calm and unflustered	**Don't** answer back or engage the caller in conversation
Disconnect or put the phone down	**Don't** become upset or *slam* the phone down
Report the matter immediately to your supervisor or to security	**Don't** hesitate to notify the police yourself if the calls continue and you are in a small office on your own

 SPECIAL NOTE

Recorded advice on how to deal with these calls is given free if you dial 0800 888777.

The bomb threat

A situation any switchboard operator dreads is receiving a bomb threat. The main rule is *don't panic*.

Try to alert someone else while the caller is still on the line	**Don't** ring off
Listen for clues – accent, background noises, approximate age	**Don't** become excited or flustered
Try to keep the caller talking (apologise for bad line etc)	**Don't** cut off the conversation or ask for caller to 'hold'
Try to find out where the bomb has been planted and the time it will go off	**Don't** throw away any notes you make about the conversation

Technology update

If a bomb threat is received by an organisation, the police need as many details of the call as possible. To help, a device is now available which attaches to the switchboard and records *all* incoming telephone calls and conversations with the operator.

After an hour the tape automatically 'loops' (so it doesn't need changing) and erases old conversations as it records new ones.

For most of the time the tape is not played back, but should a bomb threat be received, the tape is available for immediate playback to the police.

SPECIAL NOTE

The Metropolitan Police have issued a *Guide to Small Businesses* which includes an action checklist for anyone receiving a telephone bomb threat. Try to obtain a copy from your local Crime Prevention Officer.

Wrong numbers and misdirected calls

If you receive calls then inevitably you will eventually receive a call which was not intended for your organisation. This may be because:

- the caller has dialled the wrong number
- there is a telephone line or equipment fault, so that the call has been routed to you
- the caller has the wrong number noted down for the organisation he/she wants.

Do *not* become impatient or sound annoyed! Deal with the caller properly, giving your own number clearly so the caller knows where he/she went wrong. Remember – the person you are speaking to may also be an existing or future customer of your firm!

From time to time you may make a mistake and direct a call to an extension which should be dealt with by someone else. Make sure staff know the procedure for either redirecting calls or referring them back to the switchboard operator using your company's telephone system. Train your staff so they know if several calls are received then they should contact the switchboard operator to inform him/her that these calls should be dealt with by another extension – and say which one, if possible. As switchboard operator always make a note, as soon as you have been told, of members of staff who have transferred to another department or that a type of work is now dealt with by another office.

EMERGENCIES

It is very important that you know the procedure for making emergency calls. There are three main emergency services on 999 – police, fire and ambulance.

- dial the number
- state which service you require (you may need more than one)
- give the problem clearly and state your name, address and telephone number
- be prepared to give directions – use churches, pubs and other landmarks as a guide.

REPORTING FAULTS

- Dial 151 from a nearby telephone as soon as possible and report the fault. Business subscribers receive priority.
- Difficulties in obtaining a particular number should be referred to the BT operator who will check if the telephone is out of order. It may be the person has not replaced the receiver correctly after a previous call and, if so, a signal can be put on the line to remind the subscriber.
- A bad connection, eg a crossed line, will be credited if you report it to the operator immediately. He/she will also reconnect you to the number you require.

TELEPHONE SERVICES

Freefone • is easily identifiable because the word Freefone precedes the number. Freefone callers must make their calls via the operator. There is no charge for the call. Numbers prefixed 0800 are also free and can be dialled direct. Your company may have a Freefone number itself to encourage potential customers to ring free of charge.

Directory enquiries • dial 192 and give the name and town. If the name is a common one you will be asked for the initial or the address. Remember, you are charged for this service.

Information services • the only British Telecom information service still in operation on a regular basis is the speaking clock. All other information services are provided by private companies and the numbers all start with the prefix 0898. The

International • Most international calls can now be made using the IDD service. If you have a problem getting through to an international number you can call the International Operator for assistance by dialling 155.

• The tones heard on telephones abroad are not the same as those heard in the UK, and if you are about to make a number of international calls for the first time you can ask the operator to give you a demonstration of the tones you can expect to hear.

CHECK IT YOURSELF
• You can obtain a copy of the *International Telephone Guide* from British Telecom by ringing them on 0800 800 838. The call is free and so is the guide.
• It is 9 am and soon after arriving at work one of your colleagues decides to telephone your New York office about an urgent matter which has just come up. Is this a good idea and if not, why not?

TELEPHONE CHARGES AND ECONOMIES

All organisations are usually very cost conscious in relation to the use of the telephone. Most modern equipment will provide detailed printouts of calls to help reduce costs. Private subscribers can now ask for an itemised bill showing exactly how many calls were made, where to and when.

Charges are based on:

• distance (whether the call is local, national or international)
• whether the call is made at a time and day which is classified as **cheap** rate, **standard** rate or **peak** rate
• the duration of the call.

CHECK IT YOURSELF
• Find out the times and days when calls are charged at peak rate, standard rate and cheap rate.
• In discussions with your tutor and other members of your group

make out a ten point list under the heading 'Keeping Telephone Charges to a Minimum'.

- Find out the policy in your organisation (or one you visit on work experience) for making private telephone calls. If they are forbidden by a company, what facilities can be provided for employees for emergency use?

! SPECIAL NOTE

Private telephone calls are not just frowned upon because of cost. *Incoming* private calls tie up a business line and you cannot be working if you are chatting to a friend on the telephone! Try to stop anyone ringing you at work unless it's important.

PAYING FOR CALLS

For people on the move, eg representatives of a company, there are various ways in which they can pay for calls they make to their office without having to carry large amounts of change with them.

- **Phonecards** are becoming a more common method of paying for calls from a public payphone. The cards are bought for between 20 and 200 units (ie £2 to £20) units and after each call the screen on the phone shows how many units are left. Phonecards *cannot* be used in ordinary cash payphones.
- **BT chargecard.** This can be applied for by anyone with a telephone at home, as well as businesses. The chargecard is sent with a PIN number (Personal Identification Number) similar to a bank cash card. Calls are made from private phones and payphones by dialling 144 (provided the phone used is an MF phone) and then keying in the account number and the PIN. On ordinary telephones users must dial 100 and ask the operator for a British Telecom Chargecard call.

  The chargecard can also be used to make international calls via the international operator (155) and can be used to ring the UK from many countries around the world.

TELEPHONE HYGIENE

Telephones in offices are used by very many people. Some may have coughs and colds and it is important that the receivers are kept clean and disinfected regularly.

Some organisations pay for a telephone cleaning service so that all their extensions are cleaned and disinfected regularly. Even if your company does not have such a service there are many sprays on the market specially designed for the purpose and these can be used.

Do *not* use disinfectants or sprays not meant for use with a telephone as these could damage the plastic. N*ever* wash a telephone – for obvious reasons – a wipe with a damp cloth is usually all that is required for the outside.

ANSWERING MACHINES

Many organisations today use answering machines to take calls when the office is closed. Holiday booking agents often use them continuously throughout the winter months for all brochure requests. This saves tying up the main telephone lines and callers can leave their name, address and brochure request on tape, to be dealt with later.

There are two types of answering machine:
- an **answering set** – this plays a pre-recorded message but does *not* allow the caller to leave a message in reply
- an **answering machine** – this plays a pre-recorded message and then allows the caller to leave a message afterwards.

Answering machine features

Answering machines have *two* tapes. One tape holds the pre-recorded message and this automatically rewinds after every call. The second tape holds the incoming messages (normally a maximum of 90 minutes' worth) and stays in position after each message, ready for the next call.

The tape for the pre-recorded message is only short – about 3 minutes maximum – so long messages cannot be recorded for callers.

Technology update

The more sophisticated machines will allow retrieval using an MF telephone from a remote location, and can be programmed to forward a message to a specified telephone number – or even to signal a bleeper holder when a message is received.

In addition, a **keytone** device is now available which travellers can take abroad. This converts any telephone into an MF phone (simply by holding the keytone device to the mouthpiece and 'playing' it.) Therefore the answering machine can be accessed from all over the world!

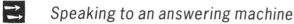

Speaking to an answering machine

Don't panic if you suddenly find an answering machine on the other end of the line! Just:

- listen for the tone telling you when to speak
- speak relatively slowly and very clearly
- give only essential facts
- spell *all* difficult proper names, using the telephone alphabet
- keep your message short – there is usually a time limit for incoming calls.

TEST YOURSELF

If it is during the winter months when you study this chapter you can do this for real!

Select a holiday brochure you would like to send for and telephone the company. Be ready to state the brochure you require (the company may issue several) and your full name, address and post code. Holiday companies also often like you to say where you saw their advertisement.

Prepare your statement in advance and practise spelling out *both* your name *and* the street or road on which you live using the telephone alphabet.

Keep your message short – preferably within 25–30 seconds.

Preparing a message

Messages should be clear and to the point. Getting the correct 'tone' can be difficult – some people sound nervous, others very formal, or too chatty.

TEST YOURSELF

You have been asked to prepare a message for your answering machine to inform callers that the office is closed for lunch until 1.30 pm but callers who wish to leave a message can do so after the tone.

1 Prepare a suitable message and check the content with your tutor.
2 Record this on tape, listen to it and comment on your own performance!
3 Now record it a second time, trying to improve any faults you had.

Listening to messages left on tape

Someone in the office has the job of listening to the tape after returning to the office, and listing all the calls and messages which have been left. This is relatively easy as you can rewind the tape to listen to any tricky parts more than once.

- Have a pad and pencil ready.
- Do one message at a time.
- Listen to it through first.
- Note the key points when you listen the second time.
- Play it through a third time and check you have it down correctly.
- If there are any queries *keep the tape intact* until they have been resolved.

Problem messages

Not all the messages you receive will be straightforward to transcribe:

- some callers may be nervous and there may be long pauses
- some may talk too quickly and be difficult to follow
- some may miss out important information
- others may talk a long time – and may even be cut off mid-way through
- some messages may require urgent action.

CHECK IT YOURSELF

Discuss with your tutor what you should do in *each* of the above situations to ensure you take, and action, the message to the best of your ability.

BLEEPERS

These are often used by people on the move so that they can be contacted quickly and easily.

There are many types available but the main choice is between:

- a sound bleeper only (Fig. 1)
- those with a numeric display (figures only)
- those with an alpha-numeric display (words and figures) (Fig. 2).

The alpha-numeric type are obviously the most expensive.

Figure 1   **Figure 2**

A sound bleeper is used for employees who work from one fixed base and therefore the bleeper signal means 'call base immediately'.

The display types can be used to give more information. To use the numeric type properly the users need to set up a series of codes so that they can identify what the message is from the code they read, eg.

0 (+ number) = ring that number
10 = call office

Alpha-numeric bleepers do *not* need a code because a short message can be sent in words.

Paging a bleeper
There are two methods of contacting a bleeper user.

- Ring the Bureau Service. Ask for the pager number and give the message – in code or words depending on the type of bleeper. The Bureau Service contacts a central computer which 'talks' to transmitters in the area. The computer is programmed with codes for each bleeper and knows which zones or regions are covered by the bleeper – therefore where to transmit to.

- Direct input. This is the same procedure but now you are talking to the computer direct. You have to use an MF phone as you enter the message with codes of figures, star and gate. At all times you are prompted in what to do by the computer voice.

SPECIAL NOTE

Direct input is the service the answering machine is programmed to use when it contacts a bleeper holder automatically.

Note that bleeper users can choose which regions and zones they want to receive from – the more they choose the more it costs.

Bleeper holders in large organisations can be contacted direct by extension users who key a special code into the phone to activate the bleeper they want. The bleeper will then display the extension number which the user must ring. This saves people having to go through the switchboard every time they want to bleep someone.

PUBLIC ADDRESS SYSTEMS

Probably the most common type of public address system is the **tannoy** system. This is wired throughout a building so that a message can be transmitted, by loudspeakers, to everyone.

Some tannoy systems automatically page people everywhere there is a loudspeaker. Other systems allow for certain speakers to be bypassed if the message has only to be sent to certain areas.

They are often used in large factories to bring people to the telephone – the usual message being 'Will Mr . . . please contact the switchboard'. Or, 'Will Mrs . . . please come to reception'. They are also often used in large hotels to page guests wanted on the telephone.

CHECK IT YOURSELF
- Why do you think a hospital would only install a tannoy system which enabled some speakers to be bypassed?

- Can you think of any other types of organisation where this would be essential?

Rules to follow

If you have to speak over a tannoy system:

- speak directly into the microphone
- speak *clearly* and relatively slowly
- *don't* shout!
- repeat the message (say it twice altogether). The first time most people miss the first bit as they only realise half way through that a message is coming over. This is especially true in a noisy workshop or factory
- give people time to respond before you send out a second call.
- *Always* check speakers to be bypassed are 'off' *before* you start to transmit!
- Some telephone systems incorporate paging systems – some PABX systems allow paging from certain designated extensions; on a multiline system the message is broadcast through the loudspeaker of all extensions not in use.

SECTION REVIEW

Having completed this section, you should now be able to:

1   State the facilities which are available on switchboard and multiline systems.

2   Explain the use of call logging equipment.

3   Identify an MF telephone and describe System X facilities.

4   Contact a car phone or mobile phone.

5   State the correct procedure for answering and connecting calls from a switchboard.

6   List the main duties of a switchboard operator.

7 Deal with difficult callers and emergency situations (including receiving a bomb threat).

8 Explain how to report faults.

9 Make international calls.

10 Identify the ways in which costs can be kept to acceptable limits.

11 Explain the importance of telephone hygiene and how routine cleaning is undertaken.

12 Use internal and external directories quickly and efficiently.

13 Leave concise and accurate messages on an answering machine.

14 Prepare a timed message and record this on tape.

15 Transcribe accurate written messages from those left on an answering machine.

16 Page a bleeper.

REVIEW QUIZ

True or False?

1 A key telephone system can support more extensions than a PABX.

2 An MF telephone is recognisable by keys with a star and a gate sign.

3 A special code is used to transmit information to a car telephone.

4 International calls are always made via the operator.

5 Callers who are 'holding' for an extension do not require attention.

Complete the blanks . . .

6 Directory enquiries can be accessed by dialling ....

7 The six emergency services accessed via 999 are ....

8 The prefix 0800 means that the call is ....

Work it out

9 Below is an internal telephone directory you have received. Change this so that it is in an order you consider would be easier to refer to.

```
Personnel Department

2114      Personnel Manager - Tom Short
2115 7    Personnel Manager's Secretary - Irene (Mrs)
          Phillips
2118      Assistant Personnel Manager - Graham Browne
2117 5    Training Officer - John Jackson
2116      Welfare Officer - Kathleen Evans (Mrs)

Sales Department

2256      Sales Manager - Mark Halstead Mary Holt (Mrs)
2257      Assistant Sales Manager - Valerie Markham
2258      Sales Manager's Secretary - Joanne Baker
2260      Sales Office Manager - Brian Bishop
2259      Sales Co-Ordinator - Ronald Wilson

Accounts Department

2349      Chief Accountant - Bob Johnson
2350      Cost Accountant - Trevor James
2351      Management Accountant - Jayne Foster (Miss)
2352 4    Accounts Supervisor - Doreen Walters (Mrs)
2353      Wages Supervisor - Sandra Adams (Miss)
```

Type out the re-arranged list on a typewriter or word processor, incorporating all the changes and amendments shown.

10 It is 2 pm on a cold Wednesday afternoon in February. Your boss wants to make several international phone calls and has asked you to look in the phone book and find out what time (and day!) it is in each of these countries at the moment:

Netherlands   Taiwan   Mozambique   Bahamas

New Zealand   Turkey   South Africa   Chile   Japan   Tonga

11 For this exercise you will need a copy of the booklet 'Your Guide to Telephone Charges', giving the latest telephone rates. This is available from your local British Telecom shop.

Your company keeps a log of all personal telephone calls

and all international calls made each month. At the end of the
period you have to cost the calls from the latest rates booklet.

Calculate the cost of each call shown below for both logs.

T MARSHALL AND CO LTD					
PERSONAL TELEPHONE CALLS					

Month March

Date	Caller	Department	Number called	Day/Time	Duration	charge
4/3	Mr V Gordon	Sales	061-239-5149	Fri 10am	3 mins	
7/3	Miss N Swift	Purchasing	071-380-2107	Mon 2pm	5 mins	
8/3	Mrs M Bolton	Canteen	34897	Tues 8.15am	5 mins	
14/3	Mrs J Cole	Sales	0772-71892	Mon 6.05pm	10 mins	
17/3	Mr S Barrett	Sales	021-289-3972	Thurs 11am	10 mins	
26/3	Mr J Sharp	Maintenance	051-734-9646	Sat 10am	5 mins	

T MARSHALL AND CO LTD			
INTERNATIONAL TELEPHONE CALL LOG			

Date	City called	Day/Time	Duration	Charge (Approx)
2/3	Melbourne	Wed 10am	4 mins	
7/3	New York	Mon 3pm	5 mins	
10/3	Paris	Thurs 2pm	4 mins	
17/3	Düsseldorf	Thurs 11am	4 mins	
21/3	Montreal	Mon 3pm	4 mins	
25/3	Istanbul	Fri 1pm	3 mins	

Section 2 – Data transmission

There are three common methods of transmitting data
electronically – fax, telex and electronic mail. All are designed to
transmit information very quickly to almost anywhere in the
world. They are therefore more expensive to use than the normal
mail service and should *not* be used for non-urgent, routine
communications.

FAX

Fax is growing in popularity almost daily as it is cheap, easy to
use and extremely convenient.

A fax machine scans a document, converts what it 'sees' to digital
signals and sends these signals down the telephone line to
another fax machine. This second machine then prints out a
replica of the original document.

The whole operation can take less than a minute, the users can speak to each other about the document on the telephone if they want, and documents can be sent quickly and easily all over the world.

Fax machines are known as **transceivers** – that is they transmit *and* receive messages. They are left in *receive* mode when not in use by the operator (on most machines this occurs automatically).

The facilities to be found on a fax machine will depend on whether it is a small, relatively cheap desk-top model or a larger model.

Desk-top models usually

- use coated paper – copies must be photocopied to last as the originals will fade over time
- may need originals feeding into the machine one by one
- may not have a manual contrast facility so that poor quality originals do not transmit clearly
- will only take A4 documents
- do not fax photographs well.

Larger models often

- use plain paper which does not fade
- have an automatic document feeder
- have an abbreviated dialling function (for frequently used numbers) and can be set to keep trying busy numbers

- will take up to A3 size originals
- have a 'half-tone' facility for photographs
- have a confidential receive mode, where documents are held in memory until they are accessed by a special user code
- will 'poll' another machine automatically at a fixed time. This means your fax calls another fax and collects any messages left for it! Useful if your fax is in Birmingham and the other is in Sydney and the time delay means you're never at work at the same time.

SPECIAL NOTE

- All fax machines come complete with an instruction manual which should *always* be used when in doubt about any procedures you want to use.
- All machines can also be set to print the fax number, name of organisation, date and time at the top of all faxes sent. You can therefore easily identify the senders of all incoming faxes.
- The layout of fax messages varies considerably. Check the format used in any organisation you work for by looking in the files.

Using a fax

Most fax machines have an LCD (liquid crystal display) which prompts you in what to do! The sequence will vary slightly depending upon the machine you are using.

You may also be offered the choice between manual and automatic transmission.

- Check first if your machine allows you to adjust the contrast so that poor quality originals still transmit well.
- Make sure the document is fit to be sent (or perhaps needs photocopying first). The first sheet needs to show the total number of pages being transmitted.
- Make sure the document guide fits the width of the document.
- Call the other fax number using the telephone.
- Make sure you are in *transmit* mode (if this is not automatic upon dialling).
- If necessary press *start* (or other assigned key) when you hear

the tone response from the other fax.
- The LCD will prompt you and also tell you if there is any fault on the line or with the transmission.
- A special bleeper sound (and/or the LCD display) will let you know if the other operator wants to speak to you.
- After use make sure the machine is back in *receive* mode.
- Most machines automatically produce a transmission report showing date and time, receiver's number, pages sent and duration of transmission. This should be attached to the office copy of the fax for reference.

CHECK IT YOURSELF

Try to get as much literature on different types of faxes as you can. Compare the features – and the prices – of each.

It is probable that any organisation you work for (or even your college or school) has a fax. Watch it in operation and send faxes yourself. When you are on work experience ask for the opportunity to send faxes.

SPECIAL NOTE
- All faxes can be used as copying machines when not in use as faxes.
- Firms usually have a *separate* telephone line (and number) for their fax – *not* the main phone line.
- The UK Fax Book is the fax directory for the UK. Directory Enquiries for numbers not listed and overseas subscribers can be accessed by dialling 153.

Fax costs

Fax is the cheapest method of sending documents electronically. The equipment is cheap – a basic business fax machine starts at about £500 – and transmission costs are the same as making a telephone call. Therefore time of day, duration of call and the distance the message is sent are the important factors. The duration of the call is determined by the amount of text and number of pages to be sent – so keeping fax messages short saves money.

Running costs are small – there is coated paper to buy for most faxes which is more expensive than plain paper. Operator costs are negligible.

The faults with faxes

Very few! The main problem is poor transmission or poor quality originals which result in unreadable faxes at the other end. Operator errors can mean the top or bottom of the document is cut off during transmission or, even worse, the fax is sent to the wrong destination!

The biggest problem for organisations is that faxes cannot be used as evidence in a Court of Law because there is no proof of the receiver's identity on the document itself – unlike telex (see below).

CHECK IT YOURSELF
Discuss with your tutor the action you should take if:

- you receive a fax addressed for another company
- you receive a fax which becomes unreadable halfway through transmission
- the operator at the receiving end signals to tell you that the fax you have just sent is virtually unreadable.

Technology update

Faxes can be used to transmit messages to electronic mailboxes (see page 35).

TELEX

Telex has been declining in popularity in the UK recently, although for companies who want to send messages to remote locations around the world it is still more likely the foreign company will be on telex than fax.

The disadvantages with telex are that it needs a typist to input the message and only text can be transmitted, not drawings, graphs, charts or photographs. The advantage is that telex messages *are* acceptable as evidence in a Court of Law because both the sender and receiver are clearly identified on both the top and bottom of the message.

Modern telex machines are very similar to word processors and many can be used as a word processor when not in use as a telex.

The message can therefore be prepared and edited on screen, stored in memory and transmitted automatically.

Each machine has its own **answerback**. This is the recognition code of each machine so that:

- the operator can check he or she is through to the correct number
- the receiver can identify who the message is coming from.

Telex layout

There is a recommended layout for telexes.

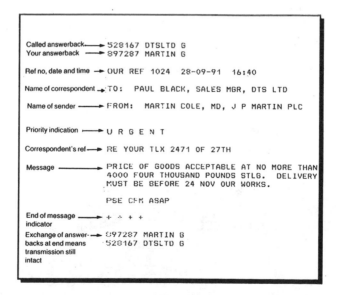

Called answerback ⟶ 528167 DTSLTD G
Your answerback ⟶ 897287 MARTIN G

Ref no, date and time ⟶ OUR REF 1024 28-09-91 16:40

Name of correspondent ⟶ TO: PAUL BLACK, SALES MGR, DTS LTD

Name of sender ⟶ FROM: MARTIN COLE, MD, J P MARTIN PLC

Priority indication ⟶ U R G E N T

Correspondent's ref ⟶ RE YOUR TLX 2471 OF 27TH

Message ⟶ PRICE OF GOODS ACCEPTABLE AT NO MORE THAN
4000 FOUR THOUSAND POUNDS STLG. DELIVERY
MUST BE BEFORE 24 NOV OUR WORKS.

PSE CFM ASAP

End of message ⟶ + + + +
indicator

Exchange of answer- ⟶ 897287 MARTIN G
backs at end means 528167 DTSLTD G
transmission still
intact

TEST YOURSELF

Have a guess (and use the Telex Directory to check) who the following answerbacks belong to:

24319 HARROD G   261209 BHSLDN G   27286 MIRROR G

265781 BBCHQ G   666322 BAWYS G   24234 SAVOY G

SPECIAL NOTE

- The letter G at the end of an answerback is the code for the UK.
- All telex messages are printed in capital letters.

SPECIAL NOTE

- The correspondent is identified clearly so that the message can be delivered promptly. This is very important if you are sending to a large organisation.
- If you are contacting someone who will not recognise your answerback give the full title of your company and the address.
- Keep the message short and free from unnecessary punctuation.
- Spell out figures (to ensure there is no mistake). Spell out fractions too, or type them as 1/2 for ½.
- Do not use the characters %, @ or £ if transmitting abroad.

Telex abbreviations

Many phrases on our sample message were abbreviated. This is to reduce transmission time (and therefore the cost of the telex).

On other occasions, abbreviations may denote a transmission problem, eg:

DER   Out of order
MOM   Wait a moment (used by operators when incoming calls are queuing)
NC   No circuits (this means the lines are busy)
OCC   The number you are calling is engaged.

CHECK IT YOURSELF

Why would you find it impossible, from your machine, to telex a firm in Russia, Saudi Arabia or China in *their* language? As a clue – the Japanese found it impossible to put their alphabet on a telex machine so . . . they invented fax!!

TEST YOURSELF

You work for DPT Computer Services Ltd, 15 Lancaster Place, Preston. Your telex answerback is 883093 DPTCOM.

Your boss, Peter Rowland, is travelling to London for an urgent business meeting tomorrow. He will be away for 3 nights and wants accommodation – a single room with bath at a good hotel.

He has asked you to:

- select a good hotel from the AA Guide
- look up the telex number in the BT Telex Directory
- telex them to see if they have a room free. He obviously needs urgent confirmation that he can stay there or else you will have to try somewhere else.

Look up the information he requires and draft out a telex using the proper layout and telex 'language'.

Check your finished work with your tutor.

Tips to help
- You should *always* give both *day* and *date* when booking accommodation to avoid errors and mistakes.
- Remember, the hotel you pick will not know your company so you must identify yourself in full.

Final point – discuss with your tutor *why* Peter Rowland prefers to have a telex from the hotel rather than verbal confirmation over the telephone.

Faults

There are few faults with telex equipment. You are unlikely to receive a telex addressed for someone else because your answerback should mean that the sender recognises he/she is through to the wrong number and disconnects.

Your main problems are likely to be with line faults – either you cannot get a line (so have to spend ages trying to get through) or the transmission cuts off part-way through. If this occurs disconnect and try again.

Many modern telex machines have an automatic transmission facility so that difficult-to-get calls can be stored in memory and the telex will keep trying to send the message automatically.

Telex costs

Dedicated telex machines are more expensive than fax machines (roughly about £2000) though these can be rented rather than bought outright. Rental costs are around £200 per quarter. Transmission costs are dearer – telex machines use telegraph lines *not* telephone lines – and access to these is more expensive, especially on the more remote international routes.

Running costs must include the cost of telex paper, which isn't expensive and an operator, who is! The fact that all telex messages need keying in first means that the time spent in document preparation is longer than with fax messages.

DELIVERY AND FILING

- Telex and fax are used to send *urgent* messages. Therefore incoming messages should be delivered immediately to the addressee.
- Original outgoing messages should always be returned to the sender for checking and filing. In the case of fax the transmission report should be attached.
- All telexes are printed with a copy, which is usually kept in the telex room for a limited period of time, filed in date order.
- In most organisations no extra copy is taken of faxes received or transmitted but this policy may vary from one company to another.

SPECIAL NOTE

In addition to sending and receiving faxes and telexes, it is also the operator's responsibility to undertake routine 'housekeeping' tasks. The most important of these is to replenish the paper when a coloured stripe appears on the roll, as this indicates that it is nearly at an end. It is the usual practice to change this immediately – to avoid the roll running out completely in the middle of an incoming message!

Check in your manual how to change the paper in your machine.

ELECTRONIC MAIL

Electronic mail is usually known as **Email** or **Elmail** for short. The principle on which it works is easy to understand.

Think of a large hotel which handles messages for hundreds of guests. The messages are kept in pigeonholes – one pigeonhole for each room number. The receptionist puts all messages received for a guest in his or her pigeonhole and gives them out when the guest asks for them (and produces identification, eg a room key).

Variations can be added to this system:

- Someone can telephone the hotel and leave a message for a guest.
- The guest can telephone the hotel and ask for messages to be given to him over the phone.
- The guest could ask the receptionist to write a comment on the bottom of a message and send both note and comment either back to the sender (via his pigeonhole if he was a guest) or to a third person staying at the hotel.
- The guest could ask the receptionist to make out a message, photocopy it and put it in several pigeonholes.
- Finally, when the guest returns to the hotel, he can check if his messages have been received (the receptionist would check the pigeonholes of the recipients to see if they were empty).

Electronic mail is based on exactly the same system. Subscribers to the electronic mail service rent a 'pigeonhole' in the form of a 'mailbox' in a central computer.

They call up this central computer from their *own* computer, send the message to another subscriber, and the computer places this message in the specified mailbox, ready for collection.

In the same way that the guest at the hotel rang in for messages, subscribers can call up the computer to check if there is anything waiting for them in their mailbox. If there is, it appears on their computer screen.

The benefits of electronic mail over telex and fax are that:

- all forms of data can be transmitted via Email – graphics, text and computer data, eg part of a spreadsheet, or a document produced on a desk top publishing package or word processor
- there is greater confidentiality as messages are only received on the computer – *not* in a central fax or telex office
- Email messages can be sent and retrieved from virtually anywhere in the world
- messages can be sent to several mailboxes at once (eg all branch offices of a company)
- the system is ideal when the final document would be put into a computer anyway before use. For instance, articles sent to a newspaper are keyed into terminals before printing. Documents received by Email are *already* in the computer system and therefore don't need keying in a second time.

Using Email

The two main Email services are **Telecom Gold** and the **Prestel Mailbox service**. Telecom Gold is the more popular of the two and has the more subscribers.

To use Email you need:

- a computer
- a telephone line
- a subscription to an Email service.

When you subscribe to Email you receive a mailbox identification (ID) number which you use as an identification number on any mail you transmit. You also receive a private password which must be used before you can gain access to your own mailbox.

- The user dials his Email service and enters his password.
- The main menu for the Email service is listed on screen.
- The user selects the service required – for instance **mail** (to send or collect any messages).
- The mail system menu is then shown on screen, eg **send**, **receive**, **scan mail** etc.
- All prompts and commands (including a help facility) are available on screen.

Additional facilities

Email services *don't* just offer the message taking/ sending service mentioned above. In addition, from the main menu users can:

- receive from/transmit to telex or fax machines
- access directories (eg mailbox numbers of other subscribers)
- contact the information services (eg on travel, accommodation etc)
- access a news screen with updated information on the service.

Email costs

To use Email a company needs a computer, modem and software to link with the electronic mail computer – there are therefore both hardware and software costs to take into consideration.

So far as using the service is concerned, Telecom Gold operates two membership schemes – Club membership for users who only require one mailbox and Corporate membership for organisations which require an unlimited number of mailboxes. The user pays an initial registration fee (which differs for each type of membership) and then a standing charge per month. Connection charges vary from 3.5p to 11p a minute depending on time of day. Additional charges are levied for sending telexes, accessing database information and other special services.

Prestel users also pay a standing charge – this time per quarter – and this is more expensive for business users than residential customers. However, there is no registration fee. Connection charges during business hours are currently about 7p a minute.

COMMUNICATING WORD PROCESSORS AND COMPUTERS

Many companies set up their own 'electronic mail' service by linking the computers in their company so that messages and documents can be transmitted from one terminal to another *electronically* – rather than printing out a document and sending it by conventional mail. This also enables branch offices to access information screens, eg diary pages for executives in the company, updated sales figures etc.

When computers are linked over a small geographical area then the system is known as a **LAN (Local Area Network)**. When the links are over a greater geographical area the system is known as a **WAN (Wide Area Network)**.

SECTION REVIEW

Having completed this section, you should now be able to:

1   Transmit and receive information by fax, telex and/or electronic mail accurately and speedily.

2   Explain the action to be taken if faults or errors in transmissions occur.

3   Describe the characteristics and uses of each system.

4   Assess each of the systems in terms of their cost and advantages/disadvantages.

REVIEW QUIZ

True or False?

1   Fax is the easiest and cheapest method of transmitting documents electronically.

2   Every Email user has their own private password.

3   The telex abbreviation DER means the number you are trying is engaged.

4   Faxes can be used to transmit messages to electronic mailboxes.

5   Drawings and photographs can be transmitted by telex.

Complete the blanks . . .

6 The abbreviation LAN stands for ....

7 The identification sign for a company on telex is known as its ....

8 The most widely used Email system is called ....

Work it out

9 Your boss was due to meet an important business visitor at Heathrow airport this afternoon – a Mr Sam McAuley – arriving by Concorde from New York at Terminal 4 at 1430. Unfortunately your boss has been delayed and will be 40 minutes late. He wants you to send an urgent fax or telex to the British Airways desk asking Sam McAuley to wait for him. Your boss's name is John Sinclair.

Draft the message *either* for fax *or* for telex and check it with your tutor.

10 Your company currently has a telex machine and your boss is considering investing in both a fax and Email, but is unsure how much each will cost him – both to set up and to operate (ie transmission costs).

Using up-to-date telephone charge leaflets and current information from British Telecom and Telecom Gold write a memo to him comparing the cost of each system.

Reception

THE ROLE OF THE RECEPTIONIST

A receptionist plays a vital role in an organisation by:

- acting as the *link* between the public and the organisation
- representing the organisation to the outside world
- having the ability to answer a wide range of queries
- coping with a variety of people and situations, often under pressure
- making sure reception is never left unattended
- never passing on confidential or sensitive information
- directing people to the right place
- making all visitors feel welcome.

First impressions are vital – a good receptionist makes visitors want to do business with his or her company, a bad receptionist actively loses customers.

CHECK IT YOURSELF

How would *you* judge a receptionist? Which of the qualities listed below do you consider the most important and why?

friendly personality	good listener	thoughtful	tactful
patient	discreet	well groomed	good organiser
good communicator	dependable	unflappable	versatile
uses initiative	loyal	accurate	good memory

Now *add* to this list any other qualities you think are important. Discuss with your tutor occasions when they will *all* be needed.

KNOWING THE ORGANISATION

A receptionist is expected to be a mine of information for everyone who calls to ask about the company, its products, services, policies and personnel. This means she needs to know about:

Organisation structure
- size, structure, branches, departments and location, personnel and who does what, internal telephone extensions

History
- background to organisation structure and operations today

Business philosophy
- company policy in relation to the community, 'green' policies, changing goods, donations to charity etc

Products and services
- whole range of products and services *plus* those not offered but which may be asked about – and where to refer queries

News
- changes in the company – promotions/transfers/new staff etc

Clients and suppliers
- regular customers and callers, where they are from, what they buy and sell, who they see.

An experienced receptionist will know most of this by heart but the *key* to always being able to help is *knowing where to find the information you need*.

SOURCES OF INFORMATION

In addition to keeping useful reference books in a reception area, a receptionist may build up a personal file containing information on the company, its products, customers and other information to help in answering the type of queries often asked.

These queries will depend very much on the type of organisation.

CHECK IT YOURSELF

What sort of specialist information do you think a receptionist working in the following organisations may need?

- doctors' surgery
- large garage
- hotel
- town hall
- vets' surgery
- solicitors

SPECIAL NOTE

In the early days a new receptionist will probably find her best source of information is *other people*. Experienced staff have a wealth of knowledge which they are usually happy to share, if asked courteously.

Reference sources

In what ways do you think a receptionist may find the information contained in or on the following useful?

- visitor's business cards
- internal telephone list
- organisation chart
- telephone directory
- company files
- company advertising literature
- AA or RAC Handbook
- company advertising literature
- *What's On* in the area
- company handbook

- office diary
- list of company first-aiders
- rail and airline timetables
- dictionary
- Yellow Pages
- company newsletters
- local street plan
- company holiday rota
- product information lists
- Hotels and Restaurants in Great Britain

CHECK IT YOURSELF

- Look through *each* of the reference books given above to see the type of information contained in them.
- Try to obtain some examples of business cards to see the information given on them.
- Remember a diary usually has several information sheets at the front! The telephone directory contains more than just telephone numbers.
- Discuss with your tutor the *additional* sources of reference available for a receptionist working in specialist organisations (see the list given at the top of the page), eg trade journals, local organisations etc.

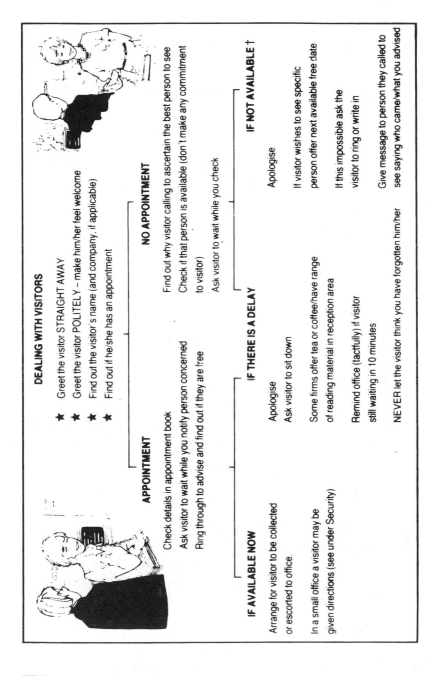

DEALING WITH VISITORS

★ Greet the visitor STRAIGHT AWAY
★ Greet the visitor POLITELY – make him/her feel welcome
★ Find out the visitor's name (and company, if applicable)
★ Find out if he/she has an appointment

APPOINTMENT

Check details in appointment book

Ask visitor to wait while you notify person concerned

Ring through to advise and find out if they are free

NO APPOINTMENT

Find out why visitor calling to ascertain the best person to see

Check if that person is available (don't make any commitment to visitor)

Ask visitor to wait while you check

IF AVAILABLE NOW

Arrange for visitor to be collected or escorted to office.

In a small office a visitor may be given directions (see under Security)

IF THERE IS A DELAY

Apologise

Ask visitor to sit down

Some firms offer tea or coffee/have range of reading material in reception area

Remind office (tactfully) if visitor still waiting in 10 minutes

NEVER let the visitor think you have forgotten him/her

IF NOT AVAILABLE †

Apologise

If visitor wishes to see specific person offer next available free date

If this impossible ask the visitor to ring or write in

Give message to person they called to see saying who came/what you advised

† If the visit is urgent and *no-one* is available to help then you will have to deal with the visitor yourself. Take down *all* relevant details, assure the visitor the matter will be dealt with as soon as possible and *pass the information on* when someone who can deal with it returns.

Difficult callers

The chatterbox
- Don't get involved! Be pleasant but 'obviously' quite busy. Don't be abrupt, just excuse yourself and carry on working.

The shy or nervous caller
- Don't become impatient or try to rush them. *Don't* finish off sentences for them! Speak gently, calmly and deliberately (very nervous people often don't 'take things in' as easily).

The angry or aggressive caller
- Stay calm and don't interrupt whilst they tell you their problem. Be sympathetic *without* accepting the blame on behalf of your company or any of your colleagues. (There are two sides to every story!) Be patient, reasonable and as helpful as possible. Get help from a supervisor if you cannot handle the situation.

The flirt
- *Don't* react – stay professional, unflustered and business-like. Remember flattery can be used to find out information from gullible staff!

Persistent callers without appointment
- Most probably reps trying to sell their products. Find out the company policy for dealing with such callers – often they are asked to write or ring the company to make an official appointment before calling.

The caller who arrives too early
- See if they can be seen *now* (especially if it's someone

important.) Otherwise make them as comfortable as possible, eg offer a drink, reading material, etc, while they wait.

The caller who arrives late

- Check if it's still possible for the person who arranged the appointment to see them – or someone else. If not, offer alternative date/time.

The VIP/pompous caller/caller in a great rush

- If you treat all callers in a friendly, welcoming way, deal with them promptly and efficiently, and try to deal with their individual needs, then it won't make any difference who they are, will it?

! SPECIAL NOTE

Don't be misled by appearance and pre-judge people! The story goes that in America a shabbily dressed man entered reception and asked to see one of the directors. The receptionist was patronising and unhelpful. It turned out to be the President of the company who had been gardening on his day off!

Golden rules

- Welcome regular callers by name.
- Remain calm and objective.
- *Really* try to help.
- Think through your decision before you act.
- Expect the best of people.

Dealing with handicapped visitors

Don't be patronising or treat people as if they are less intelligent because they have a physical handicap:

The deaf
- *look* at them when you speak to them to help them lip-read. Speak (relatively) slowly and clearly.

The blind
- speak when they enter – your voice will guide

them towards you. *Lead* (don't drag!) them to a chair. If steps, say whether they are *up* or *down* and how many there are.

The disabled
- Life will be much easier for any disabled callers if there is a ramp, rather than steps, leading to your building. Be ready to open doors if necessary. *Don't* try to rush them or appear impatient. Apart from being attentive and thoughtful and prepared to offer help when necessary, concentrate on the person, *not* the disability.

And check you know where there is wheelchair access in your building.

CHECK IT YOURSELF

What would you do if:

1 the very second a visitor arrives the telephone starts to ring?
2 a visitor calls, by appointment, and the person they are seeing is off for the day?
3 a very annoyed visitor approaches your desk to complain he has been waiting 30 minutes, whilst other people who arrived after him have already been in to see the same person he is waiting to see?
4 a visitor arrives straight from the airport with two large suitcases?

Rules to follow

- The person on the telephone *can't* see you are busy, the visitor can. Apologise to the visitor and answer the telephone. Keep the conversation brief or ask the telephone caller to hold the line a moment (whilst you deal with the visitor).
- Ask the visitor to wait whilst you check. Find someone else to help. It may be the person concerned is away ill – *never* give the impression to the visitor he/she may have been forgotten!
- The visitor concerned may have arrived very early – if so apologise and assure him/her they will be seen at the appointed time. If they have been overlooked then apologise for the delay and send them in next. *Always* keep a note of the order of arrival of visitors to prevent this happening.

- Many reception areas have a storeroom adjacent where baggage can be stored. Label it clearly (you may not be there when it is collected) – and tell the customer where you have put it (for their peace of mind!)

Car parking

A large organisation is likely to have its own staff car park with visitors' slots marked out near the main entrance. It is important that the receptionist knows the organisational procedures for reserving these spaces, though in many companies it is more a question of 'first come, first served' if parking is at a premium.

For this reason – and in case of small organisations without a car park – it is important that you know where the nearest car park or roadside parking is available. Bear in mind that visitors will not want to park where there are single or double yellow lines!

CHECK IT YOURSELF
Discuss with your tutor what you would do if, quarter of an hour after an important customer had arrived to attend a meeting with your Managing Director, a traffic warden entered your building saying that he was going to book your customer's car as it was parked on double yellow lines . . .

SECURITY AND CONFIDENTIALITY
- Many large organisations have a gatehouse where security staff check visitors as they enter the premises and issue a special visitor's badge.
- These badges may be colour-coded to show which areas the visitor has access to and which he/she hasn't.
- The gatehouse will also 'check out' visitors as they leave and retrieve their badges.
- The reception area is normally sited at the *front* of the building, adjacent to the main entrance, so visitors have no excuse for wandering about.
- In a large, security-conscious company visitors are usually escorted from one place to another.
- The reception area should *never* be left unattended and money and confidential documents should never be taken there.
- If the receptionist also operates a switchboard then there

should be a glass panel so that conversations cannot be overheard.

- Unattended bags or cases should never be left lying in reception – if so the company has the option to remove these if they are thought to be suspicious. There is often a notice in reception to this effect.
- Departments often accessed by visitors – personnel, purchasing and sales – are often sited close to the reception area.
- Do not discuss confidential matters (or gossip!) in reception, (either face-to-face or over the telephone) where you may be overheard by visitors to the organisation.

'MOVING' VISITORS

Companies vary in the methods they use to 'move' visitors from reception to the office they are visiting. Visitors may:

- be given verbal directions by the receptionist (small companies only)
- be escorted by the receptionist (providing there is still someone left on reception)
- be escorted by security staff
- be collected by the executive or his secretary.

Escorting visitors

- Walk at a reasonable pace (bear in mind the age and fitness of the visitor).
- Don't make the trip a guided tour.
- Answer general questions and let the visitor pause briefly to look at things which interest him or her on the way.
- Give warning of hazards – steps, swinging doors, congested areas.
- Show courtesy by opening doors.
- Introduce the visitor on arrival.
- If no-one is in the office when you arrive then find someone or wait with the visitor until someone comes.

Giving directions

- Be specific and clear. Don't refer to landmarks the visitor doesn't know.

- Give gestures as you talk – but make sure you know your left from your right!
- Always use left and right, *not* north and south, which is confusing.
- If the route is long make a quick sketch or write down the directions as a list of points.
- If the directions are for a journey (eg to a branch office) *start* by establishing a common point of reference in the area.
- Give landmarks such as pubs, churches and garages.
- Try to give approximate distances before turns must be made.
- If a one-way traffic system is involved try to point out one-way streets and, if turns must be made, which *lane* the driver should be in.

 TEST YOURSELF

Work out the clearest directions you can for:

- someone arriving at your organisation and visiting a room at the *opposite* end of the building.
- someone *walking* from the railway station to your local town hall
- someone *driving* from your local town hall to the railway station.

Check these with your tutor.

 ADDITIONAL INFORMATION

- Most organisations have a standard 'how to find us' package which they send to visitors who do not know the location of the organisation. These give information on
  – motorway links
  – main roads
  – parking availability nearby.

- If your own executive has to travel to an unfamiliar organisation you could ask them for details of how to get to them, parking and so on. Hopefully they will agree to send you the same sort of package!

- Whenever your executive is travelling out of town, make a note of a telephone number where he/she can be contacted. If the meeting is in a restaurant or hotel, note the name and telephone number and, if applicable, the room where they should meet (eg foyer, bar or dining room of a hotel). A brief description of the person they are meeting, if a stranger, also helps.

TEST YOURSELF

Draw up a simple 'how to find us' information sheet for your own school, college or workplace.

Note down on your plan:

- the main routes to the building
- any one-way systems a driver would have to negotiate
- local parking
- the main entrance.

What **other** arrangements do you think you may be asked to make if a visitor is travelling a considerable distance to your organisation?

GEOGRAPHICAL KNOWLEDGE

A good geographical knowledge is essential for any receptionist. Visitors travelling long distances will obviously be more tired on arrival and will welcome a polite enquiry as to whether they have had a good journey and the offer of tea or coffee.

In addition, of course, you might be expected to arrange accommodation for them. (See Arranging Travel and Meetings chapter pages 83–5).

TEST YOURSELF

How good is **your** geographical knowledge of the United Kingdom?

- Your organisation has a policy whereby all visitors who have travelled for more than three hours are offered lunch and those who have travelled for more than four hours are offered accommodation in a local hotel.

  Visitors from the following towns and cities call at your organisation this morning. List those who should be offered lunch and those who should be offered overnight accommodation, if required.

Mrs K Bradbury, Sheffield	Mr J Johnson, Taunton
Mr T Percival, Yeovil	Miss P Thompson, Wrexham
Mr L Evans, Cork	Mr K Lovell, Troon
Mr K Madeley, Nairn	Miss L Watkins, Chertsey
Mr S Chilcott, Truro	Mrs C Evans, Larne

- If you have four visitors, one from Douglas, one from St Peter Port, one from St Helier and one from Cowes, from where will *each* of them have travelled?

! SPECIAL NOTE

Receptionists are often expected to offer and/or serve tea or coffee to waiting visitors. Further details on serving light refreshments are given in the Arranging Travel and Meetings chapter (pp 102–3).

DELIVERIES

Whilst some organisations have separate entrances for deliveries to be received, in many companies it is the duty of the receptionist to deal with, or direct, delivery men and maintenance people who visit the building.

- Anyone who arrives to visit another part of the building because they are making a delivery or mending some equipment should be asked for identification.

- Be prepared to sign for goods, packets or special delivery letters received during the day. Remember that you are then accepting responsibility to make sure these get to the recipient without any delay or problems occurring!

- Anyone delivering a large item – or large quantity of goods – should be directed to the department which ordered the goods. It is not usual practice in any company to have large deliveries cluttering up the reception area – for appearance as well as safety reasons.

COPING WITH EMERGENCIES

Emergencies can occur in reception for a variety of reasons, eg:

1 A visitor is taken ill in the reception area.

2 The building has to be evacuated quickly – none of the visitors know the emergency procedures.

3 A member of staff is urgently called away – he has several visitors coming to see him that day.

4 A lift full of visitors jams between floors.

5 A visitor has his car stolen from the car park.

In some cases the organisation will have set procedures as to what must be done, ie in the case of 1, 2 and 4 above. If the organisation is large with a special security staff they will always be on hand to deal with an emergency situation.

However, in the case of incidents occurring as in point 3 above, the receptionist may have to react quickly – to find alternative people to deal with the visitors, to know who to 'put off' and who must be seen by *someone*, etc.

CHECK IT YOURSELF
Discuss with your tutor the **type** of organisational procedures which could cover 1, 2, 4 and 5 above, and what action should be taken by the receptionist.

RECEPTION RECORDS

The number and type of records kept by a receptionist will vary depending on the type of organisation and its business.

Appointments book

This is prepared in *advance* from appointments made by telephone, letters confirming appointments, information on special events etc.

The headings may vary but often include a 'comments' column for special notes and there should be room for recording unexpected visitors, if necessary.

Appointments are listed in *time* order, using the 24-hour clock.

APPOINTMENTS BOOK				
Date				
TIME OF APPOINTMENT	NAME	COMPANY	TO SEE	COMMENTS

Callers' register (or visitors' book)

This is completed *only* when the visitor actually arrives on the premises. It may be kept by the receptionist *or* by security staff at the main entrance and will probably show time of arrival *and* departure.

VISITORS' BOOK					
Date					
NAME	COMPANY	NATURE OF BUSINESS	PERSON SEEN	TIME OF ARRIVAL	TIME OF DEPARTURE

CHECK IT YOURSELF

In what ways do you think a callers' register can be used as a security measure:

- under normal circumstances
- in the event of a fire?

Staff 'in and out' book

This may be used in some organisations to record movements of staff frequently off the premises. It would also include staff absent through illness or on holiday.

Register of business cards

Business cards may be filed either under the name of the organisation or geographically, for safe keeping. They are never filed under the name of the representative, which may change.

Lost property book (see below)

Telephone index book/internal telephone directory *

Accident book

Technology update

Receptionists with a computer terminal in the reception area may benefit by:

1 Accessing **Videotext** (eg Prestel) for information they may need on travel, hotels etc.
2 Accessing a computerised appointments book/staff diary. Executives and secretaries 'log into' the computer any appointments they make and their whereabouts on a particular day. The receptionist can access any day at the touch of a button to check appointments and staff availability.

Lost property

This is usually kept in reception because visitors claiming articles they have left behind will ask for them at the reception desk.

When lost property is handed in the receptionist should:

● check to see if the article is named

● attach a tag stating when and where the item was found

● enter the following details in the lost property book
  - date
  - place found
  - description of article
  - owner's name and address (if known)
  - action taken

● either put the item into a lockable cupboard (if it is of no particular value) or try to find the owner as soon as possible. This is obviously necessary for valuable items such as credit

*Will be kept by receptionist if the job is combined with that of switchboard operator. (Further details are given in the Telecommunications chapter, pages 8–9.)

cards, passports etc. Very valuable items, with no clue as to the owner, should be handed to the police and a note made in the lost property book.

When the article is claimed the receptionist should:

- ask for identification (very important for valuable items)
- ask the owner to sign for the item claimed in the lost property book
- enter the date claimed.

Most organisations only keep lost property on the premises for two or three months unless an item is particularly valuable. Ordinary items, eg umbrellas, are often taken to a charity shop to save storage space. So that visitors will be aware of this fact, most organisations have a 'disclaimer' notice clearly displayed in reception, saying that the organisation cannot accept responsibility for any property lost on their premises.

SPECIAL NOTE

- If you ever open a purse or wallet containing money, to see if it contains any identification, **always** have a witness present. In this way you cannot be under suspicion if there is ever a query about the amount of money in it.

- If you find an unusual parcel or package or bag left behind, especially in an obscure place, it is wise to call your supervisor *before* trying to remove it. Any suspicious packages must *always* be treated with respect.

TEST YOURSELF

1 Draft out a short, clear disclaimer notice which could be displayed in a reception area.

2 a From the information given above, draw up suitable headings for a lost property book and enter the following items. Use today's date.

- a set of keys with a key tag attached stating Whitegate Motors

- A cheque card found on the floor in the Sales Manager's Office. The name printed on it is 'Mrs K Robinson' and the bank is Lloyds

- A black leather purse with zip found on a chair in the corridor outside reception. It contains £125 in cash and the only identification is the name 'G Walters' on a ticket inside.

b What action would you take in each case to try to re-unite these items with their owners?

THE RECEPTIONIST AS A MEMBER OF A TEAM

No receptionist can work in isolation but needs cover from other staff to get a drink, freshen up or go for lunch – because reception must *never* be left unattended.

CHECK IT YOURSELF
How good a 'team' member are you?

- Is your writing always legible and your record-keeping neat?
- Do you put things away in the right place after using them?
- Do you keep your records up-to-date?
- Do you expect people to drop what they are doing immediately to help you out?
- Are you punctual – if you say you will be back at a certain time, are you?
- Do you remember to give people messages and keep them informed?
- Are you quick to criticise if someone makes a mistake?
- Do you remember to thank people when they help you?

A receptionist who ignores the basic rules of courtesy to colleagues can expect little help when it is wanted!

THE RECEPTION AREA

Presentation
The reception area is usually situated near the main entrance of the building *or* at the entrance to a suite of offices. In this case the enquiry desk should be clearly indicated.

It should be bright, clean, tidy and attractive. It is the receptionist's job to:

- make sure personal articles are kept out of sight
- make sure the area itself is clean and tidy – arrange for

wastepaper baskets and ashtrays (if smoking is allowed) to be emptied regularly
- keep any stocks of magazines tidy and up-to-date
- keep record books in their proper 'home' when not in use
- file documents and keep records and files locked when not in use.

Some reception areas are comfortably furnished with armchairs and low tables, carpets and bright, modern decor. Large companies are aware that first impressions are very important and will spend thousands of pounds fitting out the area.

Some organisations design their reception area with both their company image and logo in mind, ie:

- an advertising agency may be very modern and even 'futuristic' to promote their image of being 'up-to-the-minute'

- a solicitors' office may be more traditional – to give the impression of stability and security

- the area may be decorated in the company 'colours' and receptionists may be dressed in matching outfits.

At the other end of the scale is the purely functional area in a doctor's or a vet's for example, where the receptionist may just have a glass screen and a counter to mark off appointments.

All reception areas can benefit from various additions to make them appear more welcoming.

CHECK IT YOURSELF
1 Think of reception areas you have visited. List as many items as you can think of which could be added to a new reception area, after decorating is complete and basic furniture is installed, which would make it look more attractive.
2 Now consider reception areas in large organisations where people have to spend a considerable time there, eg in a hospital. What *additional* amenities do you think could be included both in and around the reception area for the benefit of visitors?

✚ Safety first

Because of the number of visitors coming into reception it is important this is a *safe* area and accidents are kept to a minimum. This means:

- no trailing wires or cables anywhere in the area
- floors treated (or covered) so they are not slippery, even when wet
- no large panes of glass unless it is either specially toughened *or* criss-crossed with fine black wires to make it clearly visible
- chairs and other obstructions placed well away from swinging doors
- swing doors clearly marked *push* or *pull*
- fire extinguishers in the area and fire exits clearly marked.

Additions and amenities

Go back to the Check it Yourself on page 57. Here is a list to compare with your own.

Additions
- flower arrangements/plants/evergreens
- company literature
- brochures/trade magazines/periodicals (including foreign magazines if you often have foreign visitors)
- visitor's coat stand
- noticeboard with laminated notices giving information on the company which is of interest to visitors and a calendar
- wallcharts/plans/drawings/pictures
- product samples on display (if appropriate) or publicity displays
- clock (some organisations have clocks showing different world times for the information of foreign visitors)
- additional lighting in reading areas.

Plus clear notices towards other main departments eg Sales, Purchasing, Personnel.

Amenities
- pay phone (wall-mounted with acoustic hood)

- vending machines for refreshments
- public toilets
- map of building (the 'you are here' type)
- fish tank (breaks monotony, interesting to watch)
- brochures/postcards/books on sale (mainly found in hotels but some hospitals now taking up this idea).

Plus in *all* reception areas – a *first-aid box* in case of minor accidents.

CHECK IT YOURSELF
- Discuss with your tutor the contents of a typical first-aid box in a reception area and make a list of the items you would require.
- Assume you have recently taken over in reception and the manager has told you to set up a simple first-aid box but not to spend more than £15.00.
- Visit a large chemists (eg Boots) and *cost* the items you would include without exceeding the amount of your budget.

Note that no drugs of any kind would be kept in a first-aid box

TEST YOURSELF
Draw a plan to show your ideal reception area for *one* of the following organisations. Show clearly the additional features of amenities you would include:

- an architect's office
- a large school or college
- a local newspaper
- an insurance brokers

Noticeboards
- Noticeboards should be *updated* regularly.
- *Place* notices neatly and artistically – *don't* just put them up anyhow and anywhere!
- Long-stay notices should be laminated.
- Printing must be clear and neat – preferably done by means of enlarging type on a photocopier, using Letraset, a lettering machine or stencils.
- Use colour for effect but don't overdo it! Two colours per notice is enough.

- Use capitals, emboldening or underscoring for effect but again *don't* mix styles too much.
- Keep to the same style of type within one notice.
- Fasten *all* notices using the same method – coloured map pins, drawing pins or velcro. The type of fastening used will depend on the surface of the board, eg cork, fabric, fibreboard etc.

TEST YOURSELF

Your company has a rule, as part of its security policy, that management reserve the right to remove any unattended parcel or bag left in reception. Make out a clear notice to inform all visitors of this fact. Discuss the exact wording which could be used with your tutor.

Flowers and plants

Nothing looks worse in any office than dying flowers or bedraggled plants!

Flower displays

- These should be *low* if they are going to be placed in front of people or between people.
- Tall displays should be placed against a wall or in a corner
- Centre arrangements should look equally good from all angles and therefore need more flowers.
- Arrangements set against a wall are economical as flowers are only viewed from one side.
- Dried flower arrangements, displayed in attractive baskets, are long-lasting and require no maintenance.
- Larger companies, with more money to spend on floral displays, may have a contract with a local florist to supply and change floral displays weekly.

CHECK IT YOURSELF

Rather than just placing cut flowers, unimaginatively, in a vase or container, why not experiment with a simple arrangement?

Your basic materials are:

- shallow dishes

- pin holders (secured to the bottom of the container with modelling [or florist's] clay)
- oasis (different types for fresh and artificial/dried flowers)
- chicken wire (crumpled) [1"–2½" mesh] – this is placed in the top of the container or vase and holds the stems of the flowers securely upright.

Try a simple shape to start with or try copying a basic display illustrated in a book or magazine.

SPECIAL NOTE

- Top up all flower arrangements with fresh water every day.
- A piece of charcoal in a vase will keep the water clear. A lump of sugar added to water will feed flowers and keep them a little longer.

Plants

- All plants have a plastic label attached giving instructions for positioning the plant and watering. The secret is only to buy a plant which will thrive in the conditions in which it will have to live!
- Note down the instructions before you throw away (or lose) the label.
- Keep plants (and flowers) away from radiators and out of direct sunlight to prevent wilting.
- Remove plants from window sills in winter before you go home at night because of frost.
- Plants benefit from a weekly feed when they are in flower.
- Spray plants and flowers daily, using an ordinary water spray or atomiser to create humidity.
- Some companies now lease their plant displays from specialised garden nurseries who undertake weekly maintenance of the plants and will even replace them if the need arises!

SECTION REVIEW

Having completed this section, you should now be able to:

1 State the principal duties of a receptionist.

2   Describe the sources of information available to assist the receptionist.

3   Deal with routine and non-routine visitors both with and without appointments.

4   Explain how to deal with difficult callers and problem situations.

5   Explain the importance of security and confidentiality in relation to reception work.

6   Describe the correct procedure for escorting visitors.

7   Give clear directions – both verbally and in writing.

8   Complete reception records accurately and neatly.

9   Describe the interdependence of the receptionist and the importance of operating as a member of a team.

10 Explain the importance of company image in relation to reception area design.

11 Identify suitable additions and amenities for a reception area.

12 Explain the importance and relevance of safety in relation to reception area design.

13 Produce clear notices and maintain a noticeboard.

14 State the main points to be followed when creating a flower display or maintaining plants.

REVIEW QUIZ
True or false?
1   All plants need watering daily.

2   The AA handbook gives information on hotels in each town.

3   An appointments book is prepared in advance from information already known.

4   'Green' policies are those which relate to new staff.

5   A London Underground map is included in most diaries.

Complete the blanks...

6   If a visitor arrives just as the telephone begins to ring you should . . . .

7   If a visitor is still waiting after 10 minutes you should . . . .
. . . .

8   Gatehouse staff may issue . . . . to all visitors.

Work it out

9   Examine the map below carefully and work out the instructions you would give a *car driver* who wanted to travel from the Central Bus Station to the Grand Theatre.

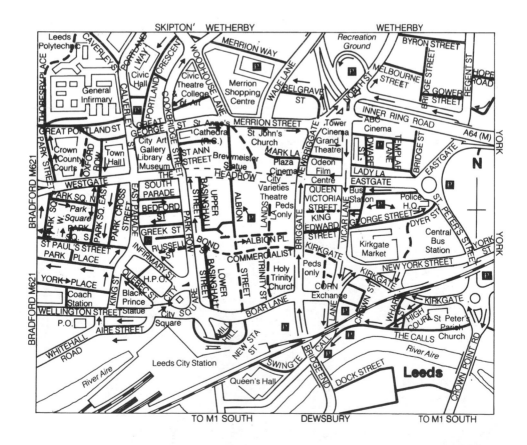

10 Draw up a reception register using the same headings as shown in the chapter. Date it for today and enter all the following appointments.

Make sure they are in *time* order, using the 24-hour clock.

3.15 pm	Mr T Williams of Aspin & Co to see Mary Thompson
10.15 am	Mr Johnson is expecting Miss Angela Dixon (interview)
2.00 pm	Mr Tyler is due for his appointment with Mrs Greenhalgh He is a representative with Acme Tiles Ltd
9.15 am	Mrs Mitchell is seeing Ms J Evans from Prospect Trading
4.10 pm	Mrs Kelly has arranged to see Mr Somerville from Baker & Cole plc.

Arranging travel and meetings

SPECIAL NOTE

This chapter gives guidance on planning and booking travel arrangements, booking accommodation, and obtaining the necessary travel documents. The second part of the chapter deals with the planning and execution of a meeting from booking the accommodation to basic procedures and documentation.

Section 1 – Arranging travel

TRAVEL

More people travel today than ever before, both on business and pleasure, at home and abroad. It will therefore be very unusual if, at some time or other you are not involved in making travel arrangements:

- to go on holiday
- for executives in your company who are travelling on business
- for people who are coming to visit your company.

Knowing the correct procedures, both for planning and making travel arrangements saves time, means there is less to go wrong and can often save money.

To be efficient you must:

- know what information you need to plan a trip properly
- have a good, basic knowledge of travel alternatives and procedures
- know which sources of information you can turn to for help
- know which agencies can help you and the services they offer
- be able to make and confirm bookings
- know the standard documentation involved
- be able to estimate the costs involved, if required.

PLANNING THE TRIP

Good planning is essential and can be more difficult for a business trip than a holiday or social occasion. This is because business trips are often made at the last minute, and arrangements may have to be changed if an emergency occurs, eg:

- another person must be included at the last minute
- another customer has to be visited in the same, or neighbouring area (or country)
- the trip has to be extended, unexpectedly, because complications arise.

Basically all planning can be categorised under four headings:

- WHERE
- WHEN
- WHO
- HOW.

These apply regardless of whether the trip is for business or pleasure.

The main consideration for a pleasure trip or holiday would probably be *cost*. Organisations too must be cost-conscious and keep their business travel within a budget, even if some of the factors they must bear in mind are different from those of a holidaymaker.

Where you go will affect:
- the currency you will require
- the documents you need (passport, visa etc)
- the language you will speak (or try to speak!)
- probably how you will get there.

Where you stay will determine:
- the quality of your accommodation
- the additional facilities on offer
- the amount of travel you will need to do to get to places you want/need to see and visit.

When you go will affect:
- the clothes you take (summer/winter)
- what you can do and see (eg special events/ public holidays)

- the time of day or night you will arrive.
- any special requests (eg travel by a specific airline).

How you go will determine:
- the length of the journey
- the amount of luggage you can take.

Every decision you make will affect the total cost of the trip.

TRAINS AND BOATS AND PLANES...

The method of travel chosen usually depends on:

- the distance involved
- the amount of time available
- the reason for the trip
- the budget available.

If you were going to Paris for a week your cheapest options would be coach or train and ferry. A plane ticket would cost more but you would arrive quicker and therefore wouldn't be as tired. For a business executive this is an important consideration, as he/she might have important meetings scheduled from the moment they arrive. For an organisation time is money, and from this point of view the quicker he/she goes and returns to the office the better.

However, the business executive who wants to visit the Continent to buy goods, and bring them back with him/her, would probably travel by car. He/she would therefore have the choice of travelling over to France by ferry or hovercraft (from Dover).

If you are planning a trip there are many modes of transport you can consider:

- private car
- taxi
- coach
- cruise liner
- hovercraft
- plane – scheduled flight
- plane – shuttle service
- air taxi

- self-drive hire car
- chauffeur driven car
- car ferry
- passenger liner
- jetfoil
- plane – charter flight
- helicopter
- train

In addition, options such as fly/drive and motorail offer dual methods of transport for one trip.

ROAD TRANSPORT WITHIN THE UK

The private car
The vast majority of people undertaking journeys every day travel by private car. Business executives may:

- have a company car – provided and paid for by the company, or
- be able to take a car from a company fleet as required, or
- be paid a mileage allowance on journeys made in their own cars.

Mileage allowances may seem generous until you realise these are meant to cover wear and tear on the vehicle as well as petrol.

Hire cars
There are many hire car firms all over the UK offering a choice between small, medium and luxury cars. To be able to hire a car you must have a clean driving licence, be at least 21 (23 in some cases), and have held a full driving licence for at least a year. The driver's licence must be produced at the time you collect the car. It is possible to hire a car for a one-way journey only, eg to travel from home to the airport. This type of service is offered by national companies who have collection points in a large number of places, including airports.

The main reasons people hire a car are:

- their own vehicle may be being repaired or serviced
- they need a special car for a special occasion
- they need a large car or a van to transport goods.

Most hire car firms also offer a chauffeur-driven service. This is usually very expensive and would probably only be used to take top executives on a journey or to meet a VIP arriving from abroad. The same type of service, although sometimes with less luxurious vehicles, is offered by taxi firms at a much cheaper rate.

Taxis

Taxis are frequently used by people without their own transport, even if only temporarily. Because of increased competition fares are usually reasonable. It is a good idea to keep a list in the office of local taxi companies who have proved reliable, reasonably priced and have good drivers in well-maintained cars.

SPECIAL NOTE

Some taxi companies also offer a chauffeur-driven service with luxury cars too. These are often hired by members of the public for special occasions, eg weddings.

TEST YOURSELF

1 Which method of transport (hire car or taxi) would you recommend as the most economical for the business executive who

- wanted to travel 30 miles from home to the airport
- wanted to travel 230 miles, visiting various customers?

2 Your boss is hiring a car for the day next Thursday. He has to make a round trip of about 450 miles.

- Car hire company A can offer him a car for £24.50 unlimited mileage.
- Car hire company B can offer him a car for £9.50 plus 3.5p per mile.

Which should he choose?

Coaches

Coaches are used mainly by ordinary travellers *not* business executives. They are a useful, cheap alternative to rail travel between most major towns and cities and often have routes where trains are not available.

Some of the express coaches, travelling nationwide, are very luxurious and have hostess service and toilet facilities on board.

Coaches are ideal for group trips as they can be hired in advance, the coach driver will stay with the group all day and often return by a route which enables most people to leave the coach as near to home as possible.

SPECIAL NOTE

You can nearly always *reduce* the price you are quoted by a company (for a taxi, hire car or coach) by ringing round and comparing prices. This is particularly true if you want one during a 'quiet' time, eg a coach in the middle of winter.

Make sure the companies you ring know what you are doing! Let them know the best price you have been given so far and see if they can beat it. *Don't* ring round indefinitely. After about four calls you should know when you have been offered a good price.

Note – *Don't* try to aim so cheaply you end up with a 'rogue' company – stick to reputable ones with good, well-maintained vehicles.

TRAVELLING ABROAD BY CAR

Visitors abroad usually want a car so that they are free to travel around within the country they visit easily and quickly. They have the option whether to:

- take their own car with them (only suitable on the Continent) and drive the moment they leave the ferry or hovercraft
- take their own car with them, travel by motorail (see under train travel) to their resort and then drive themselves (again only suitable on the Continent)
- hire a car and collect it at the airport or port.

Hiring a car abroad is similar to hiring one in this country – many of the major companies, eg Hertz, Avis and Godfrey Davis, have collection points abroad. The car can be booked through their offices in this country *or* through your local travel agent. Fly/drive holidays are package holidays where the holiday maker has a car waiting for him at the airport as part of the package offered. This is a common option on holidays further afield, eg the USA.

The regulations for British cars taken to the Continent vary from one country to another and up-to-date information can be obtained from the AA or RAC.

The driver must take with him his driving licence (in some countries an International Driving Permit is required), his vehicle registration documents and a Green Card. The Green Card is issued by his insurance company and extends his UK insurance cover to countries in Europe.

The driver should also be aware that:

- many fast roads on the Continent are toll roads
- petrol prices vary throughout Europe – it is always advisable to try to fill up on the cheaper side of any border!
- speed limits vary from one country to another and most are not the same as in Britain.

 TEST YOURSELF

1   Your boss will be travelling on the Continent by car this summer with her family. She has never done this before and is puzzling over the speed limits in various countries which are all given in kilometres per hour. You know that a kilometre is ⅝ths of a mile. Can you help her by:

a converting the following table to miles per hour

Country	Speed limit kph		
	Built-up area	Country	Motorway
Austria	50	100	130
Belgium	60	90	120
Italy	50	110	140
Netherlands	50	80	100

b can you also convert the current British speed limits to kph so that she can use these for reference?

UK	30	60	70

2 She has been told that the price of fuel in the four countries listed above varies considerably – approximately £2.00 a gallon/40p a litre in Austria, £1.91/38p in Belgium, £2.90/58p in Italy and £2.23/45p in the Netherlands. If she buys roughly the same quantity in each country, what is the average price she will pay for fuel? How could she reduce this figure?

3 Your boss wants to see as much of the Continent as possible on her travels. She intends to start the trip by visiting some friends in the Netherlands, then driving to Belgium

a which country must she now travel through to reach Austria by the most direct route?

b if she travels through Austria to Italy which *two* countries can she visit on her return journey to Britain, neither of which she has been to before?

RAIL TRAVEL IN THE UK

The busiest trains in the UK are commuter trains in and out of London and Intercity trains. Season tickets are available for those who use commuter trains every day. On other trains there are a variety of different ways in which people can travel for less than the maximum fare, eg saver tickets, family railcards and reduced rates.

The pricing system for British Rail is complicated. Basically, if you are prepared to travel when the trains are quiet you will pay less. If you travel in the rush hour you will pay more.

In addition, rail travellers have the choice between first and standard class fares, and can also make a seat reservation on

Intercity trains. A seat reservation is good value – the traveller can decide whether he wants a smoking or non-smoking compartment, facing the engine or back to the engine. He is then allocated a carriage and seat number on his ticket. Full meals are often available for first class passengers (including breakfast) and are served in a first class dining car. On some trains this facility is offered to standard class passengers if vacant seats are available in the dining car.

Sleepers are available on long journeys, eg London to Inverness. If the train arrives in what would be termed as 'the middle of the night' it stays in the sidings until a more respectable hour, so that people aren't woken up at a ridiculously early time.

Tickets can be purchased at any British Rail station and from travel agencies who are agents for British Rail. People who work for organisations where rail travel is a common occurrence may be issued with a **warrant** when they are to travel by train. The warrant represents a ticket in that it gives

- the traveller's name
- the date of departure and return
- the journey details
- the class of travel – first or standard.

However, the warrant is issued by the organisation *not* British Rail. When the warrant is handed in at the station it then goes to the British Rail offices to be priced and an invoice is sent to the organisation by British Rail for all warrants they have issued in a particular month. The system has the advantage that employees are not given money for rail travel (the fare may not be known), neither do they have to rush around buying a ticket.

CHECK IT YOURSELF
- Find out which is your nearest Intercity station. Choose a city about 200 miles away also on an Intercity line and find out

  - the price of a first *and* standard class return ticket, travelling at peak journey times

  - the cheapest price you could make the same journey for, and the difference this would make to the times you could travel.

- There are several Intercity stations in London, each serving different regions in the country. If you are in London, and want to travel to the following destinations, find out which station you would travel from

  – Edinburgh   – Isle of Wight

  – Cardiff   – Cambridge

  – Dover   – Preston

- Your boss has been in Lancashire on business and will be travelling from Preston next Wednesday morning for an early meeting in London – the time has yet to be confirmed.

  He prefers to travel on a Pullman if possible, and wants to be able to eat breakfast on the train. From the timetable below:

  – which train would you recommend and why?

  – what would be your second choice if this was full?

  – what class would you recommend he travels?

  – what would be a suitable time for his meeting to start, assuming it will take him about 30 minutes to reach the office from leaving the station in London?

INTERCITY

PRESTON → LONDON

Principal train service 2 October 1989 to 13 May 1990

Mondays to Sundays			Sundays			
	Preston depart	London Euston arrive			Preston depart	London Euston arrive
Ⓡ ●	0356	0758	C Ⓡ ●		0221	0636
Ⓡ ●	0427	0725	B Ⓡ ●		0221	0643
Ⓡ ●	0451	0746	A Ⓡ ●		0230	0653
▲ ⊠	0610	0904	C Ⓡ ●		0250	0647
▲ Ⓡ	0703	0945	B Ⓡ ●		0259	0700
Ⓡ	0703	0945	A Ⓡ ●		0259	0725
▲ ⊠	0729	1016	C Ⓡ ●		0439	0839
	0845	1135	B Ⓡ ●		0439	0851
Ⓡ ✕	0915	1204	A Ⓡ ●		0448	0914
	0945	1235	C Ⓡ ●		0506	0914
Ⓡ	0945	1235	B Ⓡ ●		0506	0916
Ⓡ	1008	1244	A Ⓡ ●		0515	0936
Ⓡ ✕	1015	1244	C		1007	1353
Ⓡ	1015	1253	B		1007	1426
	1115	1414	A		1037	1517
Ⓡ ✕	1215	1437	A Ⓡ		1235	1803
	1345	1635	D Ⓡ		1410	1801
Ⓡ	1445	1748	Ⓡ		1541	1849
✕	1545	1849	Ⓡ		1556	1916
Ⓡ ⊠	1645	1923	Ⓡ		1625	1928
✕	1715	2011	Ⓡ		1701	2014
Ⓡ	1747	2130	Ⓡ		1715	2021
	1845	2140	Ⓡ		1733	2044
	1945	2225	Ⓡ		1745	2103
✕	1945	2230	Ⓡ		1910	2206
⊢	2333	0448	Ⓡ		2017	2311
					2026	0003
			Ⓡ ⊢		2342	0448

Notes

A	Until 17 December
B	24 December to 25 March
C	From 1 April
D	From 24 December
SO	Saturdays only
SX	Saturdays excepted

All services shown in this timetable are interCity unless otherwise stated InterCity services offer First Class and Standard accommodation, light food and hot and cold drinks and reserved seats

Ⓟ	InterCity Pullman train with full meal service to customers travelling First Class
⊠	Service of meals including hot food to customers travelling First Class on Mondays to Fridays (if reserving seats in advance please indicate if you wish to eat)
✕	Service of meals including hot food to customers travelling First Class (and Standard, provide accommodation is available) on Mondays to Fridays
⇔	Service of snacks, sandwiches, hot and cold drinks available to all customers
⊢	Sleepers (also Standard seating accommodation without refreshments, unless otherwise stated). Berths may be occupied until 0700
Ⓡ	Train on which reservation is advisable
Ⓡ	Reserved seats, which are issued free of charge to holders of valid tickets, are essential for all or part of the journey
▲	OUTWARD portions of SAVER tickets are NOT valid on this train Mondays to Fridays
●	NOT an InterCity service

Refreshments are available for all or part of the journey Pullman and some other facilities may be withdrawn on Bank Holidays

For further information on train services, fards and other facilities, please telephone **Preston 59439**

The British Railways Board accept no liability for any inaccuracy in the information contained in this timetable – which is subject to alteration especially during Bank Holiday periods

RAIL TRAVEL ABROAD

Travelling by rail on the Continent is arranged through the railway organisation for the country you want to visit. Therefore if you were travelling to France you would contact SNCF (the French rail organisation) and in Germany you would contact DER (the German railway). Most Continental countries have their own rail offices in London. They will arrange connections from London to a suitable Channel port, and the sea crossing too.

It is also possible to make any of these arrangements through a travel agent, and this is certainly recommended if you want to travel by rail further afield, eg Canada or the USA.

Motorail is a European network of special overnight trains which carries passengers plus their cars over long distances. Most Continental trains, including motorail trains, have a choice between sleeper accommodation or couchettes. The first is a special compartment with bunk beds (some have private washbasins). Couchettes are cheaper – although they are in the form of a bunk bed and on some trains bed linen is provided, it is not usual to get undressed and ready for bed in a couchette compartment – for one thing passengers aren't usually segregated by sex!

There are several high speed routes in Europe – for instance between Paris and Lyon the TGV trains travel at speeds around 300 kph, reducing the journey time considerably.

SPECIAL NOTE

If ever you arrange to meet someone from a train – or be met – you *must* give the name of the station *not* just the city. This is equally true abroad. In Paris, for instance, there are many different stations – as in London. Even in other towns and cities there can be more than one mainline station.

SEA TRAVEL

Apart from ferry services, the major users of sea travel are holiday makers. Cruise liners will take passengers on round trips, passenger liners take people from one place to another. If they want they can return by sea or by air.

All major ferry services in Britain take cars and lorries. Most are known as **ro-ro** ferries (roll-on, roll-off). The cost depends on:

- the number of passengers
- the length of the vehicles
- whether sleeping accommodation is required and, if so, whether it is required with or without private facilities.

 TEST YOURSELF

1   Many ferries operate in the UK. Which country would you be going to, and which sea(s) would you be crossing if you travelled from:

- Newcastle to Bergen
- Plymouth to Santander
- Holyhead to Dun Leoghaire
- Portsmouth to Le Havre.

 SPECIAL NOTE

- Anyone travelling from Dover to Calais or Boulogne has the option of going by hovercraft rather than by ferry. The journey is much quicker, although it costs slightly more. Travellers from Dover to Ostend can go by jetfoil – a similar type of transport.
- Travellers taking their car abroad have to check in at the ferryport normally 1 hour before sailing. It can also take some time to disembark once the ferry has docked. These additional times must be allowed for when planning a journey.
- Cars must *not* be driven on to ferries with full petrol tanks. Therefore, even if petrol *is* cheaper in the UK than some countries abroad, drivers must not 'fill up' before they go on the ferry.

 ## *AIR TRAVEL WITHIN THE UK*

Flight routes within the UK are known as domestic flights and are popular with business executives who want to travel a considerable distance and return in one day.

The most common service used by business travellers is the **Shuttle** service which links the major cities in the UK with London. There is no need to book a seat on the Shuttle – all the traveller does is arrive at the airport for the flight he/she wants. Shuttles leave at regular intervals during peak times (often every hour). If one is full then the airline puts on a second plane for the 'overspill' passengers.

Other flights must be booked, either with the airline itself or via a travel agent. There is a minimum check-in time at the airport which varies depending on whether the traveller is carrying hand baggage only and/or is connecting with an international flight in London.

The minimum check-in time is given on the ticket for each flight. Organisations whose executives travel frequently by air within the UK can save time by using the Timesaver system. Either the office or the traveller can book the seat with one phone call and then write out their own ticket to present at the airport.

CHECK IT YOURSELF
Your boss will be travelling from Glasgow to London next week for a meeting to be held in the centre of the city. He wants to return to Glasgow later that day.

- What advantages do you think he would gain by travelling on the Shuttle rather than Intercity?
- Are there any disadvantages?
- Find out the price of
  – a return ticket on the Shuttle
  – a return ticket (first-class) on Intercity.
- Which method of travel would you recommend, and why?

AIR TRAVEL ABROAD
There are two types of flights for travellers going abroad:

- **scheduled** air flights, as shown in airline timetables
- **charter** flights, used by package holiday companies, where the whole plane is full of holidaymakers going on holiday to a particular destination.

Some package holiday companies may use scheduled flights for their holidaymakers, particularly for their more expensive holidays. However, the vast majority of people who buy a package holiday travel on a charter flight.

Scheduled flights are more expensive, particularly to European destinations, and are mainly used by business travellers. There are also different classes of travel, whereas on a charter flight there is usually only one class:

- **first** class – the most expensive – usually used only by VIPs
- **club** or **business** class – very popular with business travellers, especially on long haul flights
- **economy** class – the cheapest.

The differences between the three include:

- the size/comfort/spacing of the seats
- the service and type of meals offered
- the check-in procedures – first-class passengers have their own VIP lounges at airports, join the aeroplane last and leave first. Regular business travellers also have their own lounges and other advantages (see below).

CHECK IT YOURSELF
- Which aeroplane would you be travelling on if *all* the passengers were travelling first class?

Business clubs

A variety of incentives are offered to business travellers by the major airlines. Market research surveys have shown that 80% of business travellers are male, aged around 40–45, occupy a senior position in their organisation and earn a high salary. Therefore most of the incentives are targetted at this type of traveller.

British Airways operates a Club Europe and Club World to which business travellers can belong. Incentives include a valet parking service at the airport, express check-in facilities, a double baggage allowance, special lounges and business facilities at airports including workstations, telephones, fax, telex and Prestel, plus special care and attention once on board.

British Midland operates a similar system with their Diamond Club. Members have a personalised membership card and security luggage tag, can wait in dedicated lounges in UK airports and receive free newspapers and in-flight drinks.

Booking flights

Airline flights are usually booked through travel agents. However, it is usual to do a little preparation *before* contacting the travel agent if you regularly book flights for your boss.

- Most executives prefer to travel with certain airlines. You need to know your boss's likes and dislikes before you begin!
- For speed a direct connection is always better than one with connecting flights.
- You need to have at least two choices of flight when you contact a travel agent. If your first choice is full you can ask for your boss to be wait listed and, for the time being, book him on your second choice. If your wait listing comes up then the agent will cancel the second choice and notify you of the change.
- Details you need to consider are:
  – time of departure and time of arrival

  – which airport and which terminal the flight departs from/ arrives at (some cities have more than one airport, most airports have more than one terminal)

  – how much checking-in time must be allowed

  – the time difference (which can affect the day of arrival)

  – the flight number.

TEST YOURSELF

1 Airports are known in the trade by three identification letters. Some are easy to work out, eg MAN = Manchester.

Can you work out these examples?
BOM   ATH   SYD   GLA   DUB   BOS

In which country are each of these cities situated?

2 Other identification letters are less easy to work out. Some are based on the name of the *airport*, eg CDG = Paris (Charles de Gaulle airport), LGA = New York (La Guardia airport). From this, can you work out where these airports are? LGW   JFK   LHR

CHECK IT YOURSELF

Direct airline timetables are easy to follow. Look at the timetable below for direct British Airways flights between London and Christchurch (New Zealand).

- What day does the flight leave on?
- What time would you leave if you were travelling on 10 February?
- What time *and day* would you arrive? Why is the day different to the day you left?
- What is the flight number?
- How many times will you stop for refuelling?

LON

From	To	Days 1234567	Depart	Arrive	Flight number	Aircraft Stops /Class		Transfer Information Airport Arrive Depart			Flight number	Aircraft /Class
FROM	**LONDON**		**CONTINUED**									
	CHRISTCHURCH											
29 Oct–24 Jan	–3––––	1400 ④	0745‡	**BA011**	747/FJM	3						
31 Jan–24 Mar	–3––––	1620 ④	0745‡a	**BA011**	747/FJM	2						
▶	**CINCINNATI**											
	Daily	1115 ④	1908	**BA217**	747/FJM	2	PIT	1630	1810	US499	M80/FY	
	Daily	1355 ④	2215	**BA297**	747/FJM	1	ORD	1635	2010	UA444	727/FY	

a – One hour earlier from 18 Mar   d – One hour earlier from 11 Feb   Ⓝ Ⓢ Gatwick Terminals
† Next day   Ⓐ Ⓑ Manchester Terminals
‡ Two days later   ① ② ③ ④ Heathrow Terminals

Compare this with a timetable showing the same flights but assuming you start from Belfast. Discuss how to read the information with your tutor.

- What time do you leave Belfast?
- What is the flight number?
- How long do you have to wait at Heathrow before your connecting flight?

BEL

From	To	Days 1234567	Depart	Arrive	Flight number	Aircraft Stops /Class		Flight Information Airport Arrive Depart			Flight number	Aircraft /Class
FROM ►	**BELFAST CHRISTCHURCH**											
20 Oct–24 Jan		–––3––––	1030	0745‡	BA4573	757/C	4	LHR	1140	1400	BA011	747/FJM
31 Jan–24 Mar		–––3––––	1230	0745‡a	BA4593	757/C	3	LHR	1340	1620	BA011	747/FJM

1 Monday 2 Tuesday 3 Wednesday 4 Thursday 5 Friday 6 Saturday 7 Sunday
Concord · Supersonic Service F First Class J Club World or Business Class
C Club Europe. Super Shuttle or Business Class M Economy Y Economy

† Next day
‡ Two days later
$ Aircraft may vary

SPECIAL NOTE

You don't *have* to specify a return date and flight. In the case of a business trip this might not be known at the time of booking the outward flight. It is possible to travel on an **open-dated return** ticket – once the traveller knows when he (or she) will be returning he goes to his nearest airline office or travel agent in the city he is visiting and makes a reservation.

CHECK IT YOURSELF

A surcharge is an amount levied onto the final bill *after* the booking has been made, but *before* the final account has been settled. Package holidays, for instance, may be subject to surcharges if the travel company increases the price of the holiday midway through the season.
Discuss with your tutor:

- *why* surcharges may be levied

- *which* forms of travel they affect the most.

TRAVEL COMPARISON CHART

Method	Advantages	Disadvantages
PRIVATE CAR	• Door-to-door • Can commence journey/ return at own time • Relatively cheap method of travelling	• Can be hold ups through bad weather, road works, traffic congestion etc. • Parking may be difficult/ expensive in city areas • Long distances can be tiring
TAXI	• Ideal for city areas – no parking problems/ difficulties finding the address	• More expensive than private transport
COACH	• Cheap • Wide network to many areas	• Can be slow • Can suffer from traffic hold-ups
TRAIN	• Usually quite fast • Depart/arrive from one city centre to another • Fairly wide network	• May be crowded • Peak times expensive • May have to change trains on some routes • Occasional hold-ups en route
FERRY	• Relatively cheap • Regular sailings on popular routes • Accommodation available	• Slow • Can be crowded and quite noisy • Need to add 1 hour for boarding with car + at least 1/2 hour for disembarkation after docking. • Rough seas can make the journey more of an endurance test!
HOVERCRAFT	• Rapid method of transport over water • Reasonably priced • Hoverport bright and modern with good facilities	• May be cancelled in bad weather/choppy seas • Limited number of seats • Limited number of car spaces
'PLANE	• Very fast • Good facilities at most airports • Good service en route • Minimal check-in times for domestic flights	• Expensive • Airports may be situated several miles from city centre • May be delays waiting for connections • Bad weather can mean delays and/or cancellations • Baggage weight limited

ACCOMMODATION IN THE UK

Any traveller who is not returning home the same day needs to have overnight accommodation. This is usually booked and confirmed in advance – either direct with the hotel or via a travel agent.

To choose a hotel in an area you do not know means using a good reference book. Both the AA and RAC Handbooks list hotels all over the country. Another useful reference book is *Hotels and Restaurants in Great Britain*. If you need more detailed information you can contact the British Tourist Authority or the Tourist Information Office for the area in which you are interested.

Most organisations grade hotels, often into **star** categories – the more stars the more luxurious – and expensive – the hotel.

Most business executives want a hotel where:

- it is easy to park
- they can entertain important guests
- they do not have to travel far to visit organisations they have to see
- it is relatively quiet
- they can make use of services such as laundry, shoe-cleaning, hairdressing, fax and telex
- they have private facilities, a telephone and tea/coffee making equipment and supplies in their room.

Making a reservation

A reservation can be made by telephone, fax or telex. If you ring the hotel then you will be expected to confirm your reservation in writing. You are always better to ask the hotel to acknowledge the booking to you, then your boss can take proof of his booking with him when he travels.

Be careful how you ask for accommodation.

- A single room with private facilities means *either* bath or shower is acceptable. You must specify 'private bath' or 'private shower' if only one will do. (Many private bathrooms have both in larger hotels.)

- A double room means a double bed, a twin room means twin beds.
- A suite normally consists of a small lounge, bedroom and bathroom.
- You *must* specify the time of arrival if it will be later than about 1830 hours. Otherwise your boss could arrive to find the room has been let to someone else!
- Confirm to the hotel how the bill will be paid. Most business executives settle their own bill – often by credit card. The credit card may have been issued to them by their company, if so the charge will appear on the company's account. If a business executive uses his or her own card they will reclaim the amount spent on their expenses.

Don't expect a hotel to be prepared to invoice you unless you work for a large well-known organisation which has an account with the hotel.

TEST YOURSELF

Your boss, Mr T Brookes, is visiting Inverness on business and will be staying there overnight on Wednesday and Thursday of next week.

1   Use a reference book to give him an alternative of **three** good hotels and list the facilities of each in a memo.

2   Select any **one** hotel on your list and assume you have reserved a single room with private bath in his name. Write a letter of confirmation mentioning that Mr Brookes may not arrive until about 8 pm.

Check your work with your tutor.

ACCOMMODATION ABROAD

The easiest way to book hotel accommodation abroad is:

- through a travel agent
- by contacting an international hotel chain at their London hotel or office. A list of these is given in the *Travel Trade Gazette*.
- through a hotel booking agency
- by telexing a known hotel direct (not all foreign hotels have fax)
- via Prestel.

If your boss is flying by British Airways it is worth noting that they also operate a hotel booking service.

Do make sure you receive confirmation from the hotel itself and your boss takes this with him in case there are any problems.

! SPECIAL NOTE
- Make sure you check with the hotel which methods of payment are acceptable – some accept Eurocheques, some don't, some only accept one kind of credit or charge card. Make sure your boss knows how he can pay.
- Most hotels and other organisations abroad will never have heard of Access and Barclaycard! On every credit card you will find the word *Mastercard* or *Visa*. Make sure you use *these* terms when you are communicating with anyone abroad.

? AGENCIES
A variety of agencies can be contacted for different types of bookings, eg:

hotel booking agency — a list of these is given in the *Travel Trade Gazette*. There is usually no commission charged for the client for the booking – commission is paid to the agency by the hotel.

theatre booking agency — can often obtain tickets for shows which may not be available through the box office. There may be an additional charge, especially if the tickets are in great demand – do check.

visa/passport agencies — can help to obtain passports and visas in an emergency.

! SPECIAL NOTE
- Some agencies also specialise in obtaining tickets for well-known sporting events, eg Wimbledon and Ascot.
- Most theatre tickets can, of course, also be obtained by contacting the theatre. This is very easy for credit card holders who quote their name, address and card details over the telephone. The tickets are then posted to them or, if booked at the last minute, collected from the box office before the performance.

ITINERARIES

An **itinerary** is a 'programme of events' for a trip, listing travel and accommodation arrangements in date and time order for easy reference.

It may also contain information on business visits to be made and documents to be taken.

An extract from a typical itinerary for an executive travelling from Glasgow to New York for 3 days may look like this:

Mrs J Edwards – Visit to New York

TUESDAY 20 MAY

0700   Taxi from home to Glasgow airport

0745   Check in Glasgow airport (Minimum check-in time of 30 minutes for international connections)

0815   Depart Glasgow flight BA 4863   (Shuttle)

0930   Arrive London Heathrow

1100   Depart London Heathrow flight BA175

1350   Arrive New York (J F Kennedy airport)

Single room with bath reserved at the Roosevelt Hotel (confirmation attached)

TEST YOURSELF

1   Mrs Edwards leaves New York for Heathrow on Friday 23 May on flight BA 176, departing at 2100 hours and arriving in London at 0845 hours the following morning. She must check in at J F Kennedy 45 minutes before take-off. This New York flight connects with Shuttle flight BA4882 to Glasgow which leaves at 1015 hours and arrives at 1130 hours. Mrs Edwards will be met at the airport by a company car.

With this information can you complete her itinerary?

2 How do you account for the fact that *on paper* her outward flight to New York only takes 2 hours 50 minutes whilst her return journey takes her 11 hours 45 minutes?

3 What travel documents will Mrs Edwards have to take with her on her trip?

4 Look up the current exchange rate for dollars. If Mrs Edwards wants to exchange £500 sterling for dollars, how many dollars will she receive?

5 Do you consider that Mrs Edwards is making a wise decision in converting her cash into dollars for this trip? If not, what suggestions can you make?

INSURANCE

Any traveller abroad *must* make sure he or she has adequate travel insurance for cover against disasters and accidents – both minor and major – including:

- last minute cancellations
- lost luggage
- loss of money
- accidents
- inability to make the trip through strike action (eg of airline staff)
- personal liability (eg causing an accident and then being sued)
- medical problems.

It is even possible, on ski-ing holidays, to insure against no snow at your chosen resort!

Visitors to EC countries are covered for medical expenses under a reciprocal scheme but first must obtain form E111. Application forms are available at any post office. The E111 is completed only if medical treatment is obtained abroad and any fees paid can then be reclaimed. It has to be stamped in the country where treatment is obtained – so mustn't be left at home by mistake.

However, whilst the type of medical treatment obtained with an E111 is often quite satisfactory for holiday travellers, a regular business traveller may prefer to take out a more comprehensive medical insurance scheme in case he/she is taken ill abroad.

TRAVEL DOCUMENTS

Mrs Edwards needs a full passport, valid for 10 years and must obviously take this with her. For many countries a visa is also required. Under an experimental scheme this is not always necessary for visitors to the USA at present, but the situation could change.

A visa is granted, usually by the foreign embassy, to say they agree to a certain person travelling to their country *for a limited stay only*. The passport is stamped with the visa details – including the date the visa is valid from/until.

For some countries vaccinations are either compulsory or recommended, eg against typhoid, cholera, yellow fever etc. Anyone going abroad can obtain full information from their doctor on whether vaccinations are necessary.

SPECIAL NOTE

Some vaccinations should be carried out a few weeks before the trip – not left to the last minute if they are to be effective!

Vaccination certificates should always be kept safely, preferably attached to the back of the passport with a rubber band.

CURRENCY REQUIREMENTS

Wherever possible the amount of cash taken abroad should be kept to a minimum in case of loss or theft. Alternatives are:

- **travellers' cheques** These are available from banks and travel agents in different denominations and you can buy either dollar travellers' cheques or sterling travellers' cheques. For trips to the USA small denomination dollar travellers' cheques are recommended as these can be used as cash in hotels, restaurants, shops etc.

In most other countries it is necessary to cash travellers' cheques in a bank, as required. The holder must produce his or her passport as proof of identity.

When travellers' cheques are purchased they must be signed by the person who will be using them in front of the bank or travel agency clerk. A list must be made of all the numbers and kept in a safe place, separate to the cheques.

The cheques are signed once again as they are cashed. If any are lost or stolen the owner must notify the nearest bank office (he is given a list) and he will then be able to collect replacements *at no extra charge.*

- **credit cards** (Mastercard and Visa)   These are acceptable in most countries abroad and can also be used to obtain cash. Regular business travellers usually have *both* types of card as some countries/organisations are more likely to accept one than the other. Each cardholder is given a personal credit limit.

- **charge cards** (eg American Express and Diners Club)   These cards vary in that there is no credit limit *but* accounts must be settled in full each month. They are very useful for business travellers, eg for buying expensive airline tickets.

- **eurocheques and eurocard**   These are like an ordinary cheque book and cheque card. They are acceptable in many places on the Continent and in some countries outside Europe. Eurocards can also be used to obtain money from cash machines both in the UK and abroad.

CHECK IT YOURSELF
- Obtain a passport application form from your local main Post Office and discuss how you would complete it with your tutor.
- Find out the address of your nearest passport office.

✓ TEST YOURSELF

- How much would you receive in foreign currency if
  - Your boss requires £400 in US dollars and the rate is $1.82 to the pound.
  - Your boss requires £250 in German marks and the rate is DM2.87 to the pound.
  - Your boss requires £300 Italian lira and the rate is L2148 to the pound.

- If your boss returns from the US with $250 how much would he receive in sterling if the rate was now $1.79? (Remember to round your answer to *two* decimal places.)

🔑 *EXPERT HELP*

Most large organisations with executives who travel frequently have accounts with a travel agency. A travel agency will do more than just book the tickets, a good one will offer a range of services to help business travellers.

It is always wise to deal with a travel agent who is a member of ABTA – the Association of British Travel Agents – whether you are booking a holiday for yourself or making travel arrangements at work. Customers of an ABTA agency are protected if the agency gets into financial difficulties – any travel arrangements already made are honoured by ABTA.

Typical services you can expect from a travel agent include:

- general rail, air and sea reservations and tickets
- hotel reservations and voucher system
- instant travel information and booking confirmation
- special business travel insurance
- airport representation
- airtaxi or charter bookings
- self or chauffeur driven car hire
- a passport and visa service
- provision of interpreters or guide services
- provision of travellers' cheques or foreign currency
- a daily ticket delivery service

- a travel newsletter to business clients, keeping them up-to-date with new services
- individual itineraries provided with all travel documents
- good advice on cost effective travel options.

SOURCES OF INFORMATION

If, however, you still need (or prefer) to do the initial planning yourself then you do need some of the standard travel reference books to help you *plus* your own travel file. Access to Prestel is an additional bonus!

Ideally you need a copy of:

The Travel Trade Directory
- Published *annually* this contains information on all forms of travel, agencies and other specialists plus passport and visa offices.

ABC World Airways Guide
- Published *monthly* this contains timetables for all the airlines in the world.

ABC Rail Guide
- Published *monthly* this contains timetables for all rail travel in Britain.

AA or RAC Handbook
- Published *annually* these contain maps, town plans and motorway details plus information on towns and cities in Britain, hotel accommodation and garage facilities.

Hotels and Restaurants in Great Britain
- Published *annually* by the British Tourist Authority.

Hints to Businessmen
- Useful booklets covering many countries of the world and giving details of holidays, hotels, customs regulations etc. Published by the DTI.

Plus a good atlas, maps and street plans of places frequently visited.

Travel file

Your most valuable asset will probably be your own travel file – containing information you have gathered and updated and found particularly valuable.

Typical contents would include:

- British Rail timetables for routes used regularly
- airline timetables for carriers/routes used regularly
- address list of tried and tested hotels (include telex/fax numbers)
  - in frequently visited cities/towns both in the UK and abroad
  - in your own area – for visitors who are coming to see your organisation

- address lists (including telephone numbers) of
  - tourist information offices in the UK
  - tourist offices and travel centres for other countries which can provide you with useful information. (Plus, of course, any information you have received from them in the past.)
- addresses and telephone numbers of agencies which have proved helpful.

 SPECIAL NOTE

If you use any type of agency – particularly a travel agent – regularly, then it is always better to find a good one and stay with them. You can then build up a good working relationship – they get to know how they can help you best and this can improve the service you will receive.

SECTION REVIEW

Having completed this section, you should now be able to:

1 Identify the main factors to be borne in mind when planning a business trip at home or abroad.

2 Select an appropriate form of transport for a particular trip and offer alternatives if required.

3 State the advantages and disadvantages of different forms of transport.

4 Read timetables correctly.

5 Estimate costs for a business trip.

6 Select and reserve accommodation both within and outside of the UK.

7 Describe the type of agencies involved in arranging travel and booking accommodation.

8 Draw up a simple itinerary.

9 Explain the importance of travel insurance and the types available.

10 Explain the travel documentation required for foreign trips.

11 Calculate foreign currency requirements.

12 List the information sources available in relation to travel and state how these can be effectively utilised.

REVIEW QUIZ

True or false?

1 Visas are required for travelling to all foreign countries.

2 Travellers' cheques are the safest way of taking money abroad.

3 Speed limits abroad are the same as in the UK.

4 A warrant is a special method of paying for air tickets.

5 New York is the capital of the USA.

Complete the blanks...

6 Timetables for all the airlines in the world can be found in the ....

7 The two alternative ways of travelling from Dover to Calais are .... and ....

8 The 'walk-on' flights which connect London and other UK airports are called .... flights.

Work it out

9 Your boss is travelling to the following countries in Europe:

France   Germany   Austria   Italy   Spain

- What currency will he be using in each case?

- If he plans to keep his expenses to a maximum of £350 in each country, work out how much of *each* currency he can use.

Note – use the current exchange rates to calculate this.

10 You have been asked to reserve three single rooms with facilities at the Savoy Hotel, Florence, Italy. Their telex number is 570220, answerback 570220 Savofi. The rooms have to be reserved in the names of Mr T Daniels, Mrs M Bolton and Mr A Parsons who will be arriving in Italy a week on Monday and require accommodation until they leave on Thursday of the same week.

Draft the telex you would send requesting accommodation. Ask the hotel to confirm by telex as soon as possible and also ask whether payment by Mastercard or Visa will be acceptable.

Section 2 – Arranging a meeting

Meetings are held every day of the week in the business world. The vast majority are small, informal meetings where people get together:

- to discuss new plans/ideas for the future

- to be kept informed of current and new developments
- to problem solve
- to discuss/make decisions about ongoing situations
- to organise special events or occasions.

Meetings may be planned some time in advance or held at a moment's notice if an emergency develops. Some are held at regular intervals, others only when the need arises. The participants may vary – depending on the topic being discussed – or stay the same, eg a committee given the task of overseeing a certain area, eg safety.

The question of *why* the meeting is being held usually determines *who* will be asked to attend. W*ho* is to attend can often determine *when* the meeting will take place.

Types of meeting

In general, meetings can be categorised in two ways – **formal** and **informal**. The type of meeting affects the documents involved and the procedure which is followed.

Formal meetings

Annual General Meeting	must be held annually by all public limited companies. All shareholders are invited. Holding an AGM is optional for a private limited company.
Extraordinary general meetings	are called to discuss special business of concern to the shareholders.

Board meetings	are held at regular intervals by the Board of Directors of a company and headed by the Chairman.
Committee meetings	are meetings of committee members responsible for a particular area of work, eg Safety Committee or (in local government) the Housing Committee, etc.

Informal meetings

Departmental meetings	are usually held to give information to staff or discuss a particular departmental issue.
Management meetings	are meetings between managers to promote effective co-ordination of departments.
Staff meetings	are held between staff involved in a common area of work to discuss a particular issue.
Working parties	are usually set up to undertake a particular task – the members may be from different areas so that each can contribute a different type of skill or expertise.

SPECIAL NOTE

Types of committees are discussed on page 109.

Note: in this book we have used the term **Chairman** for the person who heads a company and the term **chairperson** for anyone who chairs a meeting.

Meetings procedures

The procedures to be followed at a meeting mainly depend on whether it is formal or informal.

Some formal meetings, eg the AGM, are required by law for public limited companies, and the procedure to be followed is officially laid down. Other formal meetings may be governed by the rules laid down by an organisation.

Informal meetings do not have any formal rules of procedure to be followed and rather than an official chairperson, the person who called the meeting will usually act in that role.

Meetings documents

A formal meeting will be called by issuing a formal **notice**, and this will have to be followed by a written **agenda**, listing the items to be discussed and the order in which they will be debated. Often, today, the two are combined in one document (see pages 107–8). A record of the meeting is kept in the formal **minutes** of the meeting, which are signed by the chairperson after they have been approved as being correct and accurate by all participants.

An informal meeting can be called by telephone, by memo, or by asking people on a face-to-face basis. It is usual to confirm the arrangements in writing so that no-one forgets to attend (see pages 106–7). No formal record is usually kept, although a summary of what occurred may be given to staff who attended – either in memo or note form.

ARRANGING A DATE

For formal meetings the date is usually decided well in advance, often at the previous meeting. Therefore a committee would decide at one meeting when they would next meet and anyone absent would receive this information when the official notice to attend was issued later.

For informal meetings the person calling the meeting will suggest a date on which it can be held. Ideally, especially in an emergency, several (three or four) alternative dates should be given so that the *best* date for everyone can be agreed upon.

If the meeting is being called hurriedly, and everyone will not be available at the times given, then the people involved must be divided into those whose attendance is *essential* and those whose attendance is not. People who cannot attend can be informed afterwards of any decisions reached at the meeting.

Contacting participants for an urgent meeting

If the meeting is urgent the most usual method of notification is by telephone – either to the person concerned or their secretary. You must get in touch with someone quickly who can confirm if the person concerned is free on one or more of the proposed dates.

People who are regularly out of the office can usually be contacted by bleeper or car phone if they are travelling. If they work from home or another office then it should be possible to fax them or leave a message (if necessary on an answerphone). If you have to leave a message remember to leave *all* possible dates and ask them to confirm which ones are suitable.

If all the arrangements have been made by telephone, and there is still time available, it is usual to confirm the arrangements in writing.

SPECIAL NOTE

If someone whose attendance is essential cannot attend at the last moment (eg through illness) then the meeting may have to be postponed for a few days. It is vital all participants are told *immediately* to avoid any wasted journeys and minimise any inconvenience.

Contacting participants for a non-urgent meeting

If a meeting is non-urgent it is usual to send notification by:

- memo – for an informal meeting
- notice of meeting – for a formal meeting.

Any communication about a meeting *must* include:

- the date, day and time of the meeting
- the place the meeting will be held.

There is also often some reference as to why the meeting has been called or what will be discussed.

Writing a memo

The wording on a memo is normally kept brief and to the point.

```
M E M O
TO  Linda Jenkins              REF    PK/BA
    Paul Reynolds
    Jane Walters

FROM  Peter Knowles            DATE   14 May 19--

SALES TARGETS

I should be grateful if you could attend a meeting
in my office at 11.00 am on Wednesday, 22 May, to
discuss  our proposed sales targets for the next
twelve months.
```

Make sure you include both day and date to reduce the chance of
any misunderstanding.

! SPECIAL NOTE

If a person is to be invited to attend who is not employed by the firm (eg a guest
speaker) then it is usual to:

- invite them by letter
- ask this person *first* – as often their attendance is essential for the meeting to
  take place.

The only exceptions to the 'letter' rule would be if you or your boss knew the
person well, it was essential contact was made very quickly and/or the meeting
was relatively informal.

ARRANGING THE VENUE

Who will be attending (including how many) and *when* the meeting
will be held will often determine *where* it will be held. Meetings
may take place

- in someone's office
- in a special meeting room
- in the board room
- in a committee room
- in a special suite or room in an hotel.

Internal venues

Not all organisations have committee rooms. Those that do are likely to be local authorities, health authorities etc where there are many committees in operation, holding frequent meetings.

Many organisations do have a board room where more formal meetings are held, and this may be used if it is free or if many people will be attending.

A small, informal meeting will most likely take place in someone's office or in a small, spare room kept for meetings.

If the room is used by different people for different meetings it may have to be booked in advance. This can be done by:

- putting a notice on the door to reserve it for that date
- contacting whoever is responsible for the room and 'booking' it for that date.

SPECIAL NOTE
- Make sure the room is free *before* you send out any notification of the meeting!
- If you have to book it for a specific period of time make allowance for the meeting running on a little eg book 1 hour, not 45 minutes.

External venues
A company may arrange to have their meeting at an external venue, eg a hotel if:

- a large number of people will be attending
- the meeting will be held 'out-of-hours' eg in the evening or at the weekend.

Many hotels have special rooms or suites of rooms which can be hired for a fixed period. They will organise for equipment to be available, if required, and meals or light refreshments to be served at pre-arranged times.

TEST YOURSELF
You work for the Sales Manager, Geoff Ingham. He has asked you to write a memo to all Area Sales Managers asking them to attend a meeting at 2 pm, two weeks today to discuss the new national advertising campaign. He wants you to use the words *New Advertising Campaign* as your heading.

Bearing in mind that you have reserved the board room for the meeting to take place, as there are ten Area Sales Managers, write the memo he requires. Mr Ingham expects the meeting to last about 3 hours.

Check your work with your tutor.

ADDITIONAL ARRANGEMENTS

The type of additional arrangements required will depend on many things – the length of the meeting, who will be attending, what the meeting is about and so on.

A general check list would include:

- booking equipment – flip charts, overhead projector, slide projector, video, tape recorder etc
- arranging parking – especially if important people are travelling a long way by car
- arranging refreshments – normally tea/coffee and biscuits but a buffet may be required if the meeting goes on over a meal time
- door sign – this usually says *meeting in progress* or something similar and prevents interruptions
- maps – a *how to find us* pack might have to be sent to people who have never been before
- messages – any phones in the room must be diverted whilst the meeting is in progress. A list of people attending must be given to someone who can take messages on their behalf and the switchboard informed
- accommodation – may be required for people coming from out of town
- paperwork – any papers or documents required for the meeting must be prepared in advance
- miscellaneous items – include paper, pencils, ashtrays, water and glasses etc
- reception – should be informed who is expected and when.

TEST YOURSELF

1   Bearing in mind the length of Mr Ingham's meeting (see page 100), the people attending and the subject of the meeting, which of the above arrangements do you think you will have to make to ensure the meeting runs smoothly?

2   Now put your jobs in the order in which you would do them.

3   On the basis that participants should always be informed of arrangements in advance, which of the above should be included in your memo:

   a   for the benefit of those who are travelling a long way?
   b   for those who will be giving a talk or presentation at the meeting?

4   Add an additional paragraph to your memo to include this information.

Catering arrangements

These vary from one organisation to another. You may be expected to:

- liaise with the catering section – if this is the case there may be a standard form to complete to order refreshments
- contact outside caterers and obtain quotations
- assist in the preparation of simple buffet food yourself.

Even if the refreshments are provided by a catering section you could easily be involved in having to serve them to participants.

SERVING LIGHT REFRESHMENTS

Tea and/or coffee may be served during small or large meetings, at interviews and on several other occasions. Ideally, visitors should be given a choice between the two – "Would you like tea or coffee?" – and not just offered one which they may not like.

Check *beforehand* whether visitors like their tea or coffee black or white – don't presume everyone takes milk. If a guest wants coffee, put coffee in *first*, then add milk or cream if required. If you are pouring out tea, put the milk in the cup first and *then* add the tea, unless of course the tea is preferred black.

Serving small numbers

Always use a tray to carry the cups and saucers. Put a spoon on each saucer and serve sugar separately in a sugar bowl containing its own spoon. It is always easier, if the room is nearby, to pour out the drinks beforehand if you can.

Serving large numbers

The best way is to have a large coffee pot and tea pot (or urn) situated on a side table in the room. You should always:

- check with the chairperson *before the meeting starts* what time he/she would prefer the refreshments to be served

- check again at the appointed time that it is in order to serve (this warns everyone to make room for the cups!)

Ideally two people should be 'on duty' – one putting the drinks in the cups whilst the other takes them to the visitors. Place sugar centrally on the table and have enough sugar bowls (about one for every six to eight people.)

SPECIAL NOTE

- Don't lean over people as you are serving.

- Place a cup to a person's right side.

- Make sure all the cup handles also point to the right as you place them down.

- Never overfill cups so that the tea or coffee spills into the saucer! If this happens exchange the saucer for another.

- If you serve biscuits or sandwiches too, then make sure these are arranged attractively on plates. Allow one large plate to about six people for biscuits and four people for sandwiches. Have side plates available so that people don't get crumbs everywhere.

- Don't forget to return later to clear everything away – usually when the meeting is over.

COUNTDOWN TO A MEETING

You can rank the jobs you have to do into five sections:

1 **When the meeting is first suggested**
Contact everyone involved with the proposed date(s).

Check room is free for agreed date (or find alternative location).

Confirm meeting in writing (if sufficient time) and include any documents people must study before the meeting.

2 When the meeting is arranged

Book any equipment required.

Book any accommodation required for people from out of town.

Send maps to those who may need them.

Arrange refreshments.

3 The day before

Type list of those attending and give to reception.

Arrange for someone to take messages (you?).

Arrange parking availability.

Collect together any meeting documents, spare paper and pencils.

4 On the day

Put notice on room door.

Check room is tidy and has ashtrays (if smoking is allowed), water and glasses.

Check there is enough seating and that heating and ventilation are adequate.

Give any telephoned messages of apology to the person who called the meeting.

Check equipment is in room and, if electrical, is functioning correctly.

Check catering arrangements.

Check switchboard operator knows where calls should be diverted.

Put any telephones in the room on divert.

You may be asked to greet the visitors as they arrive, attend the meeting yourself or serve refreshments. (If you are involved in either of the last two activities you obviously can't take messages as well!)

5 After the meeting

Collect any documents left in the room.

Make sure cups/glasses are cleared away.
Type any documents recording what happened at the meeting, as requested.

TEST YOURSELF

The Production Manager of your company is in an important meeting with the Managing Director, the Personnel Manager and two Union representatives discussing industrial unrest in the factory. There is talk of a strike ballot being held in the works unless the management agree to increase the current pay offer. You have been told they must not be disturbed and have been asked to take messages. What would you do if:

- the Production Manager's husband telephones and, despite everything you say, insists that she phones him back immediately about an urgent matter.
- a reporter from the local paper phones asking to speak to either the Managing Director or the Personnel Manager or the Production Manager. When you say they are in a meeting, he asks what the meeting is about.

Interruptions

It is always difficult to know what to do when there is an urgent message for someone who is in a meeting and does not want disturbing. What to do can depend on:

- how long the meeting is scheduled to last
- how long it has been underway.

If it is expected to end soon then you may be able to wait until it is over and, the minute it has finished, find the person concerned and give them the message.

If you have no alternative but to interrupt the meeting then the way to do this is to knock, enter quietly and pass a written message unobtrusively to Mr X – so that the other participants will not know the content.

Confidentiality

The discussions which take place at most meetings are confidential in one way or another. Comments may be made about:

- members of staff
- systems of work

- competitors, suppliers and customers
- plans for the future.

If you are invited to attend a meeting you must *never* disclose anything that is discussed to anyone who did not attend. If you are discussing anything that was said with someone else who attended the meeting, be careful where you do this as you may be overheard. As you become more experienced you will be better able to judge what can be mentioned and what can't, but remember – the first time you talk out of turn will probably be the last time you are asked to attend!

If you are asked over the telephone to disclose what a meeting is about, the best thing to do is to pretend ignorance and say you don't know. This way you can't be 'pumped' for information.

SPECIAL NOTE

Confidential documents should be:

- kept in folders and labelled confidential
- kept locked away when not in use
- distributed on a restricted access basis only, i.e. numbered and only given to people on an authorised list.

Draft copies should be shredded when no longer required.

KEEPING A RECORD OF EVENTS – INFORMAL MEETINGS

If a very informal meeting is held between a small number of people on a general topic then it is possible that no formal record of what took place will be kept.

If the meeting is important then some note of what was decided is usually held

- to keep senior members of staff informed about events
- so that the notes can be referred to in the future if there are any queries
- to remind people what they agreed to do at the meeting.

eg

```
MEMO

TO    Suzanne Carter              REF       AW/BD

FROM  Andrew Walker               DATE 6 June 19__

ULTRAFORME PLASTICS LTD


At the recent meeting held to discuss the fact that
Ultraforme are rumoured to be considering giving their
next large order to one of our competitors, it was
agreed that Ennyd Blanford and I shoud visit Bryan
Heys, their purchasing manager, as soon as possible.



Arrangements have now been made for us to go there
next Wednesday, 11 June and I will keep you informed
of the outcome.



cc Ennyd Blanford
   John Dimitris
   Brenda Turner
```

SPECIAL NOTE

If you have to type a memo which has to go to several people, and the names won't fit on the top, type a distribution list at the bottom and tick off the names.

MEETINGS PROCEDURES AND DOCUMENTATION – FORMAL MEETINGS

Notices and agendas

Whilst the date for a formal meeting is usually agreed in advance, at the previous meeting, it is always confirmed in the notice and agenda sent out nearer the date. The notice gives details of where and when the meeting will be held.

In many organisations this, too, will be set out in a memo but the wording will be slightly more formal.

The agenda is a list of the items which will be discussed at the meeting and usually includes several 'fixed' items which occur at the beginning and the end of the meeting. In the middle are the main items of new business to be discussed.

```
MEMO

TO     Safety Committee      REF     MW/KE

FROM   Mike Williams, Chairman DATE 20 May 199_

SAFETY COMMITTEE

The next meeting of the Safety Committee will
take place in the Board Room at 10 am on
Tuesday, 4 June 199_.

AGENDA

1   Apologies for absence

2   Minutes of previous meeting

3   Matters arising from the minutes

4   Safety Officer's Report

5   Fire drill procedure

6   Accident figures for January - March

7   Any other business

8   Date and time of next meeting
```

Fixed Procedures { 1, 2, 3

Main Business { 4, 5, 6

Fixed Procedures { 7, 8

Fixed procedures

- **Apologies for absence** – people who could not attend
  should have notified Mike Williams (or his secretary) with
  their 'apologies' so that time is not wasted waiting for them
  to appear.
- **Minutes of previous meeting** – the members check that the
  minutes (official record of what happened) at the last
  meeting are accurate.
- **Matters arising** – if anyone was asked to do anything or
  check on anything at the last meeting then progress on this is
  discussed.
- **Any other business** – if people want to discuss minor items
  not listed on the agenda – now is their chance. (Important
  items should be referred to Mike Williams for inclusion on
  the agenda.)
- **Date and time of next meeting** – this is agreed whilst
  everyone is present and a mutually convenient date can be
  arranged.

SPECIAL NOTE

- Spare copies of the agenda should be kept for the meeting – in case anyone has forgotten their own copy.
- A permanent committee (eg a Safety Committee) is called a **standing committee**. A committee which is formed only on a temporary basis (eg to organise a special event) is called an **ad hoc committee**.
- The technical term used for calling a meeting is **convening** a meeting. We could therefore say that Mike Williams, chairperson of the Safety Committee has convened a meeting for the 4 June.

Minutes

Minutes are the official record of what took place at more formal meetings. They also include a list of everyone who was present. Notes for the minutes might be taken by the chairperson or the secretary. A copy is sent to all the people who should have attended – whether they did or not.

At this stage you would not be expected to write the minutes of a meeting though you may be asked to type them from handwritten notes. The example on page 110 should give you an idea of what to expect and the type of layout used.

SECTION REVIEW

Having completed this section, you should now be able to:

1   Identify the main types of formal and informal meetings.

2   Make arrangements for formal and informal meetings to be held at internal and external venues.

3   Notify participants correctly regarding details of the meeting and arrangements made.

4   Describe the type of documentation required for both informal and formal meetings.

5   Explain the correct way to interrupt a meeting.

6   Explain the importance of security and confidentiality in relation to meetings and how this is achieved.

eg

heading gives details
of WHAT, WHEN and WHERE →

chairman listed first →
all other members listed
in alphabetical order

minutes are always written

IN THE *PAST TENSE* and

IN THE *THIRD PERSON*

MINUTES OF THE SAFETY COMMITTEE MEETING HELD AT
10am ON TUESDAY, 4 JUNE 19__ IN THE BOARD ROOM

Present

Mike Williams (Chairman)
Katriona Abbott
Jane Knowles
Peter Salam
Karen Turner

APOLOGIES FOR ABSENCE

Apologies were received from Kevin Doughty and
Corinne Fletcher.

MINUTES OF PREVIOUS MEETING

The minutes were taken as read and accepted as a
true and accurate record.

MATTERS ARISING

There were no matters arising

SAFETY OFFICER'S REPORT

This was very favourable, the only criticism was
that the fire doors were persistently wedged open
on the first floor. Peter Salam agreed to raise
this matter with the sales manager whose staff
occupy this area.

FIRE DRILL PROCEDURE

The last fire drill had been held on Monday, 27 May
and the building had been cleared in 2 mins 30 secs.
As this was an excellent time no changes were
proposed to the existing procedures.

ACCIDENT FIGURES FOR JANUARY – MARCH

These were excellent. Only two minor accidents had
been reported during this period.

ANY OTHER BUSINESS

There was no other business.

DATE AND TIME OF NEXT MEETING

The next meeting will be held at 10 am on
Tuesday 6 July in the Board Room.

Minutes are always signed →
and dated by the Chairman

Signed .... (Chairman)

Date   ....

True or false?

1 All meetings are held at regular intervals.

2 An agenda is a list of items to be discussed at a meeting.

3 A message for someone who is in a meeting should always be given verbally.

4 A committee formed on a temporary basis only is called a standing committee.

5 Minutes must always be signed by the chairperson.

Complete the blanks . . .

6 The official term for calling a meeting is .... a meeting.

7 Three items of equipment which may be required at a meeting are ...., ... and ....

8 A list of those people present at a meeting (with the exception of the chairperson) is always typed out in .... order.

Work it out

9 Your boss, Patrick Maguire, the Sales Director, wants to hold a Sales Presentation Meeting with all Sales Representatives four weeks today. Your company has fifteen Sales Representatives who live all over the country.

The meeting will start at 1.30 pm and continue until 10 pm with a break of one hour between 5.30 pm and 6.30 pm and Mr Maguire would like to hire a room for this at the nearby Swan Hotel. The aim of the meeting is to familiarise all representatives with the new product lines for next year.

a List the arrangements you will need before the meeting takes place and the facilities you will require at the Swan Hotel.

b Draft a letter to the Manager of the Swan Hotel enquiring if a room, and the facilities you require, are available on the required date, and submit this for Mr Maguire's approval.

c Assuming the Swan Hotel has now confirmed the booking, write a memo to the representatives informing them of the meeting and the arrangements you have made.

10 You have recently been nominated as chairperson of the Student Committee for your college (or school). Draft a notice and agenda to all the other student representatives informing them that the first meeting will take place in the Student Common Room at 11.30 am on Thursday next.

The items to be discussed at this meeting are the adoption of a student charity for the year, the Christmas disco and a proposal for a student payphone.

(Note – because this is the *first* meeting to be held of the Student Committee you can ignore the first three standard items which are normally listed on an agenda.)

Processing payments

Section 1 – Petty cash

 Petty cash is the amount of money kept in the office to cover small day-to-day items of expenditure. The amount kept in petty cash is enough to cover expenditure for a week or a month. (The word 'petty' means small.)

Examples of petty cash expenditure

- A manager returns to the office from the station by taxi.
- The receptionist is told to buy flowers for the reception area.
- The milkman needs paying for milk delivered to the organisation.

Any employee who spends money on behalf of the organisation will obviously want paying back and this is done through petty cash.

 ## THE IMPREST SYSTEM

This is the most widely used petty cash system.

- At the beginning of the petty cash period the petty cashier is issued with a float, or **imprest**, of an agreed amount, say £200.
- At the end of the period the total expenditure is calculated and balanced with the amount of money remaining.
- The petty cashier is then reimbursed with the money which has been spent, to restore the float to its original amount.

The petty cashier therefore starts every new petty cash period with the same imprest (float) amount.

The benefits of the imprest system

- It is easy to check.
- Expenditure is analysed.

- It limits outlay to a fixed sum.
- Sufficient money is always on hand.
- Increased demand for petty cash is quickly noticed and action can be taken (either by reducing expenditure or increasing the imprest.)
- It minimises work for the Chief Cashier.
- It links the petty cash system to the main Cash Book and accounts records.

The job of the petty cashier

Busy cashiers, in charge of thousands of pounds, do not want to be bothered with requests for small amounts of cash. It is therefore usual for a responsible member of staff to be put in charge of the petty cash float.

The petty cashier:

- is responsible for getting the float from the cashier initially
- keeps the money safely locked away in a strong petty cash tin
- makes sure that a petty cash voucher is completed every time money is spent. The voucher shows the reason for payment and is signed by the member of staff as they are repaid. The petty cashier also signs it to acknowledge it is correct and has been passed for payment

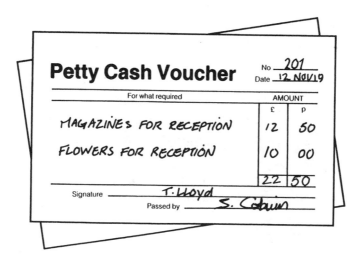

- attaches any official receipts, obtained by staff as proof of purchase, to the matching voucher
- sorts the vouchers into numerical order and enters these *daily* into the petty cash book. This book has analysis columns which correspond to the organisation's Ledger accounts. The different types of expenditure are therefore entered under a category heading, eg travel, stationery etc.
- files the vouchers in date and numerical order
- regularly checks to make sure that the total amount spent *plus* the amount of money remaining *equals* the amount of the original float
- balances the petty cash book at the end of the petty cash period and calculates the total amount spent on petty cash
- claims this money back from the chief cashier (who will usually check the petty cash book) so that the imprest is restored.

Security
- The petty cash tin should be
  - locked away when not in use
  - never left lying unattended.
- Strict control must be kept on the petty cash payments otherwise it is easy to lose small sums of money through loss or fraud.
- To help prevent fraud all vouchers *and* the petty cash book pages are *numbered*.
- When the vouchers are recorded into the petty cash book the number on the voucher is also entered. Any that are missing are therefore easily noticed.
- All vouchers *must* be passed or authorised before the money is paid out.
- The petty cash book is verified as correct by the chief cashier at regular intervals.

PETTY CASH AND VALUE ADDED TAX
Organisations which are registered for VAT can reclaim the money paid out in VAT on petty cash expenditure. To keep a record of this a separate VAT column is shown in most petty cash books.

For VAT to be reclaimed a VAT invoice *must* be obtained from the supplier. Only suppliers registered for VAT themselves can issue such an invoice. The invoice must show both the supplier's VAT Registration Number *and* the tax point of the invoice.

On a VAT invoice the amount, the item cost and the amount of VAT are usually shown separately. The price of the item is then entered in the petty cash book in the appropriate analysis column, the amount of VAT under the VAT column and the total amount spent in the total payments column.

Remember that *no* VAT is levied on travel (eg train fares, taxis etc), on food, books or magazines. The most common item in petty cash expenditure where VAT can be reclaimed is petrol. Garages usually issue VAT *inclusive* invoices or receipts so that the amount of VAT which has been paid must be worked out first.

VAT inclusive accounts

In some cases the amount paid on an account is *inclusive* of VAT, eg petrol. If an expense claim is submitted for a VAT inclusive item then the amount of VAT has to be calculated so that it can be recorded separately.

Calculating VAT on inclusive accounts
to work this out use the following formula:

$$\frac{\text{rate of VAT}}{\text{VAT rate} + 100} \times \text{amount spent}$$

To see how this works, imagine a representative has spent £88 on petrol. VAT is 15%.

$$\frac{15}{15 + 100} = \frac{15}{115} \times 88 = £11.48$$

You can cancel down the fraction $\frac{15}{115}$ to $\frac{3}{23}$ to make things even easier.

Calculating the exclusive price

This is carried out either by subtracting the amount of VAT you have just worked out from the total paid (£88 − £11.48 = £76.52) or using the following formula:

$$\frac{100}{\text{VAT rate } + \ 100} = \tfrac{100}{115} = \tfrac{20}{23} \times \text{amount paid}$$

This is a better system as it gives you a double check on your first figure, as obviously the VAT + the exclusive price must equal the total amount.

✓ TEST YOURSELF

Calculate the VAT and the exclusive price on each of these amounts (to two decimal places)

1	£65.55	**2**	£97.75	**3**	£35.65
4	£17.63	**5**	£64.50	**6**	£22.60

Changing VAT rates

The formula will operate even if VAT rates changed – all you need to do is substitute different figures, eg if VAT went up to 20% the formula to calculate the VAT would be:

$$\tfrac{20}{120} = \tfrac{1}{6}$$

✓ TEST YOURSELF

Calculate the cancelled down formulae if VAT was lowered to
1 5%   **2** 10%

! SPECIAL NOTE

Never 'guess' whether VAT should be listed separately. If you are in *any* doubt at all, *always* check with a supervisor.

CHECK IT YOURSELF

When you are at work or on work experience:

- find out the amount of petty cash kept in the company
- find out the main items of expenditure
- compare the type of voucher used with the example overleaf
- find out if your organisation is registered for VAT.

✓ TEST YOURSELF

In each of the following cases a representative is claiming back money spent on petrol. Calculate the VAT in each case:

Mrs J Black	£16.50
Mr T Edmunds	£24.85
Mr L Malik	£17.20
Mrs M Walker	£29.40

eg *Petty Cash Book example*

Sarah Arshad is petty cashier at Merrivale Electronics. Her petty cash float is set at £400 per month. During February she passed vouchers for:

1 Feb	petrol	£15
3 Feb	coffee	£3.50
5 Feb	petrol	£45
8 Feb	visitor's buffet lunch	£52.25
8 Feb	return train ticket	£85.30
15 Feb	tea	£1.75
17 Feb	stationery	£27.00 + £4.05 VAT
19 Feb	art materials for display	£18.20 + £2.73 VAT
23 Feb	sandwiches	£14.75

The following shows her petty cash book for this month.

DR   PETTY CASH BOOK   CR

RECEIVED	DATE	DETAILS		TOTAL PAYMENTS	VAT	Travel	Books + Stationery	Entertaining	Office Sundries
£400.00	1 Feb	Balance	b/d						
	"	Petrol	131	15.00	1.96	13.04			
	3 Feb	Coffee	132	3.50					3.50
	5 Feb	Petrol	133	45.00	5.87	39.13			
	8 Feb	Buffet lunch	134	52.25				52.25	
	"	Return train ticket	135	85.30		85.30			
	15 Feb	Tea	136	1.75					1.75
	17 Feb	Stationery	137	31.05	4.05		27.00		
	19 Feb	Art materials	138	20.93	2.73				18.20
	23 Feb	Sandwiches	139	14.75				14.75	
		TOTAL		269.53	14.61	137.47	27.00	67.00	23.45
		Balance	c/d	130.47					
£400.00				£400.00					
130.47	1 March	Balance	b/d						
269.53	"	Cash received							

- Note the entry of each item under its appropriate analysis heading and the total column.
- VAT has been calculated on petrol and entered in the VAT column.
- The only other times VAT has been entered is where it was *specifically* listed.

BALANCING THE PETTY CASH BOOK

To balance the Petty Cash Book you must ensure that the following processes are carried out.

- All the analysis columns have been totalled.
- The total payments column is also totalled and this is cross-checked against the total of *all* the analysis columns and the VAT column added together.
- The balance carried down must equal the amount of money remaining at the end of the month.
- When the cashier restores the imprest this is also recorded.

> **CHECK IT YOURSELF**
> Work through this example carefully with your tutor. Make sure that you understand *every* entry and the way the balancing has been carried out at the end of the month.

TEST YOURSELF

You work as petty cashier for a company which is registered for VAT and are issued a float of £500 per month. Your vouchers for this month are

Date	Voucher No	Item	Cost
1 May	120	Coffee	£6.30
3 May	121	Papers	£3.50
5 May	122	Taxi	£14.50
8 May	123	Petrol	£32.50 (VAT inclusive)
10 May	124	Train fare	£63.00
15 May	125	Petrol	£36.70 (VAT inclusive)
18 May	126	Stationery	£43.70 + £5.70 VAT
23 May	127	Buffet	£47.20
27 May	128	Reference books	£37.50

Head analysis columns as shown on the example. Draw up the petty cash book on 31 May and show the restoration of the cash to the imprest amount on 1 June.

SPECIAL NOTE

- Do remember to *cross-check* the total of all the analysis columns with the total payment column.
- If you don't balance then you will have to find your error. Do this *methodically* by:
  - counting all the entries to make sure you haven't missed one out
  - checking you have entered all the figures correctly
  - checking you have entered each item *twice* – once in the *correct* analysis column and once in the total payments column
  - checking that if the item contains VAT, the figure in the analysis column plus the VAT figure equals the total payment entry
  - checking your additions.

  Don't give up and ask for help without trying to find the error yourself!
- Use the example on page 118 to help you balance off correctly.
- Don't forget to carry down your new balance and add the money received to restore the imprest.

PETTY CASH AND THE MAIN ACCOUNTS

There is a close relationship between petty cash and the main accounts. Every organisation records payments in and out of the bank and payments made in cash in a **Cash Book**. Cash transferred to the Petty Cash Account is therefore entered as going *out* of the Cash Book (an entry on the credit side) and *in* to the Petty Cash Book (an entry on the debit side.) Note that you have been entering money received at the DR (debit) side of the Petty Cash Book.

At the end of the petty cash period, the total amount of expenditure under each analysis column must be posted to the correct expenses account in the General Ledger (eg Travel, etc.)

So that the system is easy to follow, **folio references** are used to indicate exactly where each amount of money has been posted from or posted to. This reference indicates the accounts book and page number, therefore CB12 would be Cash Book page 12, GL10 would mean General Ledger page 10. Often there is a separate folio column for this purpose.

On the following page is shown the same petty cash exercise which was used as an example on page 118. This time a folio column has been included and folio references written in. Note that these are written *underneath* the analysis columns where they refer to totals transferred to the General Ledger.

The Cash Book entry for the beginning of the month is also shown so that the relationship is easy to see.

DR	Cash £	Bank £	Cash Book	Cash £	Bank £ 400·00	Page 12 CR
			1 Feb Petty Cash			

PETTY CASH BOOK

RECEIVED	DATE	FO	DETAILS	VCHR NO	TOTAL PAYMENTS	VAT	TRAVEL	BOOKS & STATIONERY	ENTERTAINING	OFFICE SUNDRIES
£400 00	1 FEB	CB12	BALANCE	b/d						
	"		PETROL	131	15·00	1.96	13.04			
	3 FEB		COFFEE	132	3·50					3·50
	5 FEB		PETROL	133	45·00	5·87	39.13			
	8 FEB		BUFFET LUNCH	134	52·25				52·25	
	"		RETURN TRAIN TICK	135	85·30		85.30			
	15 FEB		TEA	136	1·75					1·75
	17 FEB		STATIONERY	137	31·05	4·05		27.00		
	19 FEB		ART MATERIALS	138	20·93	2·73				18·20
	23 FEB		SANDWICHES	139	14·75				14·75	
			TOTAL		269·53	14·61	137·47	27·00	67·00	23·45
			BALANCE	c/d	130·47	GL6	GL10	GL23	GL31	GL63
£400·00					£400·00					
130·47	1 MARCH		BALANCE	b/d						
269·53	"	CB12	CASH RECEIVED							

SECTION REVIEW

Having completed this section, you should now be able to:

1 List the duties of the petty cashier.

2 State the benefits of the imprest system and how this operates.

3 Withdraw money from the main cash account for the imprest.

4 Make payments from petty cash against correctly authorised vouchers.

5 Describe the relationship between VAT and petty cash.

6 Correctly enter petty cash expenditure into analysis columns, including expenses with VAT.

7 Accurately balance the petty cash book and reconcile cash held.

8 Describe the security procedures necessary in operating a petty cash system.

9 Explain the relationship between petty cash records and other accounts records.

REVIEW QUIZ

True or false?

1 Petty cash is for large items of expenditure.

2 At the end of a fixed period the petty cashier is reimbursed with the money which has been spent.

3 VAT is levied on all expenditure.

4 Vouchers are filed in alphabetical order.

5 Vouchers must be countersigned by the petty cashier when they are passed for payment.

Complete the blanks ...

6 The formula for calculating the VAT inclusive amount when VAT is 15% is ....

7 The total amount spent to date and the amount of money remaining must always equal ....

8   The system whereby the petty cash opening balance is the same at the start of each period is known as ....

Work it out

9   You are the petty cashier at Foyle Plastics Ltd. Your imprest is £500 per month.

Make out the Petty Cash Book for the month of April, using the following analysis columns (in addition to a VAT column):

Stationery   **Travel**   **Postage**   **Office Sundries**

You have been away ill for the past few weeks and, when you return, you find that your stand-in has not made any entries for the month. In addition, the vouchers are muddled up, both in terms of date and voucher number.

Sort out the voucher entries, shown below. Enter these correctly. Your organisation is registered for VAT so you should calculate how much VAT is involved in any petrol expenditure.

Balance off the petty cash book at the end of the month and restore the imprest on 1 May.

Date	Voucher No	Item	Cost
13 April	379	Plane ticket	£89.50
28 April	384	Window cleaning	£26.00
05 April	376	Charity donation	£15.00
16 April	380	Registered letter	£2.65
24 April	382	Petrol	£22.50
08 April	377	Plant for reception	£8.50
05 April	375	Stationery	£32.00 + £4.80 VAT
13 April	378	Train fare	£52.60
22 April	381	Coffee	£6.50
28 April	383	Telephone cleaning	£22.55 + £3.38 VAT

Section 2 – Receiving and recording payments

Organisations will receive payments in many different ways depending on the type of goods and services they provide.

The methods of payment used by customers will often depend on whether payment is made just once or over a period of time.

TYPES OF PAYMENT

In all the above cases payment is only being made *once*. Therefore the most likely methods are cash, cheque, credit card or postal order – although not all would be acceptable in each case.

When something is being paid for over a long period of time, eg a car, a house or services such as electricity or gas, it is easier to use one of a range of services provided by the commercial banks.

All payments, whether they are received through the post, over the counter or via the banking system *must* be recorded accurately so that the information can be transferred to the correct accounts.

Mistakes can result in:

- annoyance, inconvenience and worry for customers
- a considerable amount of work for the accounts staff who have to find the error.

CASH PAYMENTS

All businesses which receive large amounts of cash daily use cash registers (tills) to record the payments and issue receipts. Every item is also printed automatically on an audit roll which is used to check every transaction through each cash register. A sales analysis can easily be achieved by allocating certain keys for certain types of sales and this is also printed on the record. The total for the day should obviously agree with the till return showing the money received. Any discrepancies should be noted and signed for by a senior member of staff, with the reason given, if known.

Technology update

The latest electronic cash registers:

- automatically calculate and display the change required
- are linked to the stock control system – the operator either keys in the stock number *or* uses a bar code reader to automatically enter the stock code
- fully itemise all purchases on the customer's receipt
- may automatically check credit cards and print individual sales vouchers
- can even print the name of the company and the amount of the payment on the customer's cheque.

Handling cash

- You will usually be given a **float** in the morning. This is an amount of cash to enable you to give change easily even at the start of the day and will contain a mixture of coins (and maybe some notes). The amount of the float will vary, depending on the organisation.
- Check any money you receive *carefully* – watch out for foreign coins or tokens.
- *Always* count out the change to the customer. This acts as a check for them and a double check for you.
- If the till you are using does not calculate change automatically, place *notes* on the shelf above the till drawer (some tills have a special clip) whilst you get out the change. This prevents you forgetting whether the customer gave you a £5, £10 or £20 note – and also prevents anyone claiming to have given you a larger note than they actually did.

- If you are not using a till then the money received *must* be recorded on a payments inwards sheet. The design of this form will vary depending on why you are receiving the money.
- The total amount received during the day must be balanced with the total on the form or the till.

SPECIAL NOTE

The term **legal tender** means that the money is legally acceptable in payment. Scottish banknotes and Northern Ireland notes are both legal tender in England just as Bank of England notes are acceptable in those countries.

Technically, too large a quantity of coins can be refused as being not legal tender – more than £10 in 20p or 50p pieces, more than £5 in 10p or 5p coins and more than 20p in copper coins. In reality few organisations would refuse in case they lost a sale.

CHECK IT YOURSELF
Find out the largest denomination bank note issued by:

- the Bank of England
- the Bank of Scotland.

Written receipts

Customers who pay in cash often expect a receipt as proof of payment. Usually these are issued automatically by tills. Even in organisations which do not use a till it is usual to give a receipt – this time on a special form. Customers may specifically request a receipt, particularly if they wish to claim the money back from someone else.

The design of a receipt can vary. Small receipt books can be purchased with the headings printed on. Organisations may design their own to link to the type of payments being made.

SPECIAL NOTE

- Receipts designed to cope with large cash payments normally show the amount in *both* words and figures, as a double check.
- Receipts are always made out in *duplicate* so that the company also has a copy for its own records.

DUGDALE & YATES LTD

The Vehicle Bodyshop
Aberdare Road
CARDIFF
CD4 7JS

RECEIPT
No. **147**

RECEIVED FROM ... *J Donovan*

the sum of ... *Thirty-two pounds*

£32-00

in payment of ... *Replacement side window*

Received by ... *Katherine Edwards* .... Date ... *14 May 19—*

PAYMENTS BY CHEQUE

There are *three* parties to any cheque:

- the **payee** – the person or company named on the cheque to receive the money
- the **drawee** – the bank from which the money is drawn
- the **drawer** – the person making out the cheque who will be drawing the money out of their account.

Crossed cheques

Today most cheques are printed with two vertical lines down the centre. This means the cheque is **crossed** and therefore *must* be paid into a bank account. It cannot be cashed over the counter and is therefore safer if it is lost or stolen.

> **CHECK IT YOURSELF**
> Study the example on page 128 and find the name of the drawee and the drawer and where the payee's name would be written. Identify the vertical lines which mean the cheque is crossed.

Note the different numbers printed on the cheque and why they are used.

Note the different numbers printed on the cheque and why they are used.

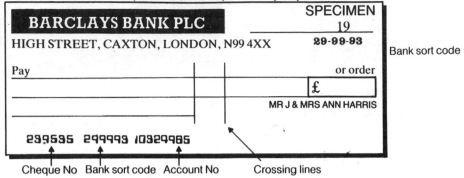

BARCLAYS BANK PLC

SPECIMEN

19

HIGH STREET, CAXTON, LONDON, N99 4XX

29-99-93

Bank sort code

Pay _____ or order

£

MR J & MRS ANN HARRIS

239535   299993   10329985

Cheque No   Bank sort code   Account No   Crossing lines

Checking cheques

Before accepting a cheque in payment the details must be checked carefully.

- The date must be accurate.
  - Early in a new year people often write the wrong year by mistake.
  - A cheque more than 6 months old is not valid.
  - *Never* accept a post-dated cheque – one made out for a later date than the date payment is being made.
- The payee's name must be correct. Many organisations have rubber stamps which they use to save the customer writing it in. In other cases the correct *official* title of the organisation is shown on a printed notice for people to copy.
- The amount in words and figures *must* agree.
- Any alterations must be initialled by the drawer.
- The signature must be the same as the specimen kept for that account by the bank. (See notes on cheque cards below.)
- The cheque should be written in blue or black ink.

SPECIAL NOTE

- The amounts should be written to the left of the lines to make alterations or additions difficult if not impossible.
- The amount of *pence* can be written in figures throughout.
- Any remaining blank spaces after the amount in words should be cancelled by drawing a line through them.

BARCLAYS BANK PLC

HIGH STREET, CAXTON, LONDON, N99 4XX

SPECIMEN

31 September 19 9–

29-99-93

Pay   J. Goodman + Co. Ltd   or order

Four hundred + twenty seven pounds -73   £ 437-73

MR J & MRS ANN HARRIS

John Harris

299595 29 9993 10329985

Cheque cards

Most private individuals are asked to produce a cheque card
when they pay for goods by cheque. The amount on the card can
vary, although the usual amount is £50. The card *guarantees* the
cheque for the amount shown on the card.

When you are shown a cheque guarantee card you must check:

- the signature on the card – it must match that on the cheque
- the expiry date on the card – to check it is still valid
- the bank sort code on the card – it must match that on the
  cheque.

The cheque card serial number is then written clearly on the back
of the cheque. Most organisations would also expect you to
initial the back of the cheque too, and some organisations also
ask for the customer's address.

SPECIAL NOTE
Many banks issue the same card for a variety of purposes, eg cash card, cheque
card, debit card. The words *cheque guarantee* may therefore **not** appear on the
front of the card you are offered, but on the reverse.

CREDIT CARD PAYMENTS

The most common credit cards in use today are **Access** and **Visa**
cards. They are accepted by many organisations including

garages, shops, restaurants and hotels and this fact is normally advertised in the window or near the counter.

If you are offered a credit card in payment you must check that the card is acceptable and seek authorisation when necessary. There are two ways of doing this.

Authorisation

The traditional method

All organisations have a **floor limit**. This is the maximum amount they can accept before they make a special check. The agreed floor limit may be as low as zero or as high as £500.

Above the floor limit a telephone call is made direct to the credit card company who run an immediate check through their computer to ensure the card hasn't been stolen and is not over the credit limit. If there are no problems they issue an **authorisation code** which is entered onto the voucher. This guarantees the payment.

The new method

The advent of new technology has meant considerable changes in the handling of credit cards:

- the card number is entered onto a special terminal linked to the credit card companies
- the card information is transmitted 'down the line' and automatically checked by computer
- if the check runs smoothly then a sales voucher is automatically printed by the terminal for signature by the card holder
- If the check shows a problem, eg that the card is stolen or the customer has exceeded his credit limit then a referral is made for further information and investigation. The method by which this is carried out may vary depending on the terminal used.

SPECIAL NOTE

Many organisations – especially retail stores – have their own sales vouchers for use with the normal credit cards *and* their own store cards. The information from these vouchers is extracted by the store and then transmitted electronically, rather than the vouchers themselves being processed.

Sales vouchers

Where sales vouchers are not issued automatically by a terminal, the sales vouchers for the appropriate credit card must be made out by hand.

The details from the credit card itself are transferred onto the voucher by means of a special imprinting machine.

The voucher is then completed by the sales clerk and the customer is asked to sign it. The signature *must* be checked with that on the card and the expiry date on the card must also be checked carefully. If you make a mistake destroy the voucher and start again – don't alter the shop copy – it *must* be identical to the customer's copy.

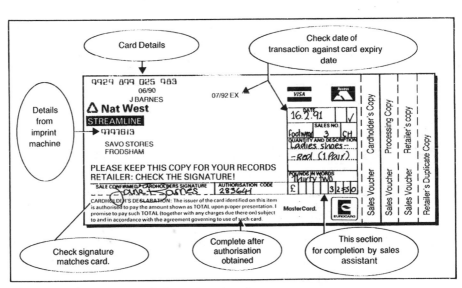

There are *four* copies of the sales voucher:

1 top copy – given to the customer
2 second copy – for the credit card company. This is paid into the bank
3 third and fourth copies – kept by the retailer (for at least 6 months).

Within 5 banking days of making out the vouchers, the company must complete a Voucher Summary Form which lists all the vouchers and take it and the vouchers to the bank for reimbursement.

It used to be the case that there was one type of voucher used for Visa transactions and a different type used for Access. Now retailers use a smaller type of sales voucher (see example above) for both types of transactions. This means there is only one voucher summary form to complete and all the vouchers – regardless of whether they are for Visa or Access cards – can be taken to the same bank.

SPECIAL NOTE

- Under the new computerised terminal system there is no need for the retailer to deposit any vouchers at the bank. The top copy issued is given to the customer and the duplicate issued by the terminal is kept by the retailer.

  Because the credit card company computer has already checked and logged details of the transaction the money will be credited direct to the retailer's account.

- When credit card payments are being made by telephone, eg for theatre tickets, holiday deposits or mail order goods, the customer does not sign a voucher. The clerk receiving the call notes the customer's name and address, card number and the expiry date of the card. They can then carry out an acceptability check before issuing the goods or tickets. The voucher is usually sent by post as confirmation.

TEST YOURSELF

1   The following customers each offer a £20 note in payment. How much would you give in change if they had bought goods worth

   £6.47   £13.23   £19.20   £14.89   £11.96   £5.05?

2   How much money will you have received altogether if, in addition to the cash shown above, you have also received four cheques for £56.20, £18.03, £32.65 and £128.94?

CHECK IT YOURSELF

Did you know that credit card companies *deduct* a percentage from the payment they make to retail organisations as their commission? Following a recommendation from the Monopolies and Mergers Commission organisations can now charge different prices, if they like, for goods bought by cash and goods bought by credit card.

- Do you think organisations will be more apt to *reduce* existing prices and offer discounts for cash or *increase* existing prices to charge extra for goods bought by credit card, and why?

- Many organisations are against the idea of introducing a dual pricing system. Can you think why?

TECHNOLOGY UPDATE

A new option for paying is by **debit** card, eg Connect or cards under the Switch system. When these are put through a till linked to the EFTPOS* system the money is automatically transferred out of the holder's bank account and into the payee's bank account over the next three working days.

SPECIAL NOTE

It may be the case that you are asked for credit by a customer (ie he wants to take the goods and pay for them later) because:

- he hasn't enough money with him

- he has forgotten his cheque book or credit card

- he knows your boss well/has had credit before.

Never agree to anyone taking goods without paying without specific authorisation from your supervisor – no matter what he or she tells you!

RECORDING PAYMENTS RECEIVED

Payments received may be listed:

- by type of *payment* (cash, cheque, credit card)   *or*
- by type of *sale*.

PAYMENTS INWARDS ANALYSIS				
Date	Total Amount Received	By Cash	By Cheque	By Credit Card
4 March	16. 50	16.50		
"	39. 40		39.40	
"	8.00	8.00		
"	55.80			55.80
"	16.30		16.30	
"	73.00			73.00
"	21.80	21.80		
TOTALS	230.80	46.30	55.70	128.80

*   Electronic Funds Transfer at Point of Sale

The listings may also include:

- remittances received through the post (though these may be recorded in a separate remittances book)
- payments made to service and delivery men or representatives, and brought into the office.

SECURITY

Organisations dealing with large amounts of cash have to take a variety of precautions:

- tills or cash drawers must be emptied *regularly*
- all money taken must be given to the cashier and locked in a properly mounted, fire-proof, wall or floor safe. (Some organisations have large 'walk-in' safes.)
- large organisations will have a safe which requires a minimum of *two* keyholders to open and lock it
- a burglar alarm will be fitted on the premises. This may have a direct line to the burglar alarm company who will contact the police if the alarm is activated
- staff who collect money when they are outside the premises, eg servicing staff, should *always* be required to give a numbered receipt to the customer
- staff who handle large amounts of cash should be vetted and their record-keeping checked
- large amounts of cash should not be kept on the premises overnight
- the company should be properly insured for any cash remaining on the premises.

CASHING UP

The correct way to cash up is to:

- separate cash and cheques
- list the cheques and add these up
- separate the bank notes according to denomination. Make sure the Queen's head is uppermost and to the right on each (they are easier to count this way)
- count the notes – first for £50, then £20, £10 and £5 and note down the amount *separately* for each denomination

- count pound coins into £10 piles – they should all be the same height! Put any coins left over alongside
- count 50p coins into £5 piles – again any left over should go alongside
- 20p coins are counted into £1 piles
- 10p and 5p coins can be mixed together – put into £1 units
- put 2p coins into piles of 10p *plus* 1p coins into piles of 10p
- total all the coins – again keeping denominations separate – £1 coins, 50p, 20p, remaining silver, all bronze coins.
- add the total of the cash received (notes plus coins)
- add to this the total of the cheques received.

! SPECIAL NOTE

By dividing the notes and coins up in this way it is easy to double check your figures afterwards by counting *each* different denomination separately and ticking this off your list.

The final information is easy to transfer on to a bank paying-in slip.

Remember – Although you add up to the number of coins (or notes) you list the **total** amount on your list – therefore 4 × £20 notes = £80.

✓ TEST YOURSELF

How much altogether have you received if your cashing up results in

3 × £20 notes	6 × £10 notes	27 × £5 notes
16 × £1 coins	5 × 50p coins	19 × 20p coins
8 × 10p coins	19 × 5p coins	60p in bronze (2p and 1p coins)

! SPECIAL NOTE

If you have opened with a float remember that this must be *deducted* from your total to find your net takings.

If your float this morning was £35 what are the net takings for the exercise above?

◁ *SECTION REVIEW*

Having completed this section, you should now be able to:

1 Explain why all payments received must be recorded promptly and accurately.

2 Receive cash payments and count out correct change.

3   Cash up at the end of the working day and balance money received against takings and initial float issued.

4   Explain what is meant by the term **legal tender**.

5   Correctly complete receipts.

6   State which components on a cheque must be checked before it is accepted in payment.

7   Explain the function of a cheque card and the components which must be checked.

8   Accept payment by credit card, use the correct authorisation procedures and operate a credit card imprinter.

9   Differentiate between a debit card and a credit card and explain the term EFTPOS.

10   Explain how to deal with requests for credit.

11   List the security procedures to be followed when handling cash.

12   Explain the implications of different methods of payment.

REVIEW QUIZ
True or false?

1   Bank of Scotland notes can be spent in shops in England.

2   The drawee of a cheque is the person who signs it.

3   A cheque is no longer valid if it is over 3 months old.

4   The maximum amount of a cheque card is always £50.

5   The bank sort code appears twice on a cheque.

Complete the blanks . . .

6   The term .... means that notes and coins can be used to buy goods in the normal way.

7   Two vertical lines drawn or printed on a cheque mean it is

....

8 A post-dated cheque is one which is ....

Work it out

9 Draw up a payments inwards sheet and list the following payments you have received today, under *type* of payment. Total the sheet and cross-check your figures.

By Cash – £13.85   £42.30   £2.45   £6.80   £9.76   £14.20

By Cheque – £34.80   £42.10   £113.80   £23.67   £50.02

By Credit Card – £34.50   £52.91   £102.56   £83.94

10 How much will you have taken altogether today if your cashing up results in:

6 × £50 notes	53 × £1 coins	29 × 5p coins
7 × £20 notes	17 × 50p coins	31 × 2p coins
23 × £10 notes	22 × 20p coins	16 × 1p coins
14 × £5 notes	19 × 10p coins	2 French francs

Section 3 – Routine banking transactions

DEPOSITING MONEY AT THE BANK

To avoid large sums of money being kept on the premises, takings should be banked regularly. A very large organisation may employ a special security company, eg Securicor, to transfer the money. Even a small organisation should bank their takings quickly and use the night safe if the bank has closed by the time they have cashed up. Any cash left on the premises must be locked away in the safe.

SPECIAL NOTE

Organisations with cash registers usually leave the till drawers *open* at night (and obviously empty) to prevent them being forced open if there is a break-in.

Transporting money

- Cash should be placed in special plastic bank bags before being taken to the bank. The bags are different colours and hold different denominations of coins (eg £20 in £1 coins). It does not matter if the bags aren't full but banks object strongly to bags containing mixed coins.

- Staff should *never* be asked to carry large amounts of cash to the bank – especially on a regular basis. If you *are* asked to do so (and it would create problems to refuse) then the very least you should insist on is someone to accompany you.
- If you regularly take small amounts of money to the bank then vary your route and the time at which you go.

Bank procedure

The bank will check the amount of money you hand over – they count notes and weigh bags of coins.

They will tick each entry on the paying-in slip (for details see below) as they check it.

If all is correct they will initial both the paying-in slip and the counterfoil (or duplicate) and date stamp it. Do check this is done (banks do make mistakes!). The cashier will keep the top copy of the paying-in slip and return the book to you.

If there is a minor discrepancy the cashier will ask if you agree this and then amend your paying-in slip accordingly. If the error is a major one, you will be given everything back to sort out yourself.

SPECIAL NOTE
- When money is being cashed up and a paying-in slip prepared, cheques and postal orders should be *re-checked* to make sure they are completed properly and not out-of-date.
- *Don't* try to pay any foreign coins into the bank – they will be rejected. If you accept any in error it is your loss.

CHECK IT YOURSELF
- Money can now be paid into the bank at automated deposit machines. These are usually situated *inside* the bank and are useful if the counters are very busy. See if you can see one in your local branch and watch it being used.
- See if you can see the night safe at your local bank. Find out the procedure for companies who wish to use this facility.

Paying-in slips

Whenever money is taken to a bank a paying-in slip is completed. This lists the payments received, divided into cash and cheques.

On the back of each paying-in slip there is space to list the drawers of cheques and the amount of each cheque. The total of this is carried forward to the front and added to the cash total. A *separate* list of all cheques should also be kept by the company in case there are any queries.

The cash must be analysed, ie divided into different denominations. The example below has been completed by a cashier who had the following:

2 × £50 notes	7 × £1 coins	17 × 5p coins
7 × £20 notes	11 × 50p coins	17 × 2p coins
6 × £10 notes	7 × 20p coins	12 × 1p coins
23 × £5 notes	9 × 10p coins	

In addition the cheques have been listed on the reverse and the total carried forward. (Postal orders are also listed with cheques – in exactly the same way.)

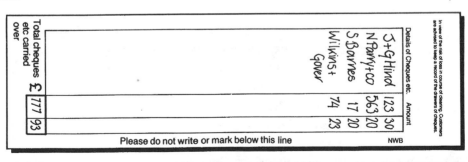

✓ TEST YOURSELF

Complete a paying in slip for your company, JTS Services Ltd, and date it today. Your takings are:

2 cheques – £183.45 (Mrs A Brand) £63.40 (Mr B Henry); 1 postal order – £40.50 (Miss S Walker)

Cash –		
1 × £50 note	13 × £1 coins	15 × 5p coins
15 × £20 notes	22 × 50p coins	13 × 2p coins
5 × £10 notes	17 × 20p coins	3 × 1p coins
16 × £5 notes	6 × 10p coins	

❗ SPECIAL NOTE

- If you make a mess of a paying-in slip (eg when working out your cash analysis), *don't* take it to the bank. Cancel it clearly and neatly write out another one.
- Paying in credit card vouchers and making out a voucher summary form are dealt with on pages 131–2.

🔑 *WITHDRAWING CASH FROM THE BANK*

Private individuals can take money out of their accounts by:

- cashing a cheque
- using the cash machine.

Cash machines are in service 24-hours a day and, in addition to obtaining cash, users can order a statement, a new cheque book or ask for the balance of their account.

Each user is given a **PIN** (personal identification number) which he or she must *remember* and not write down! In addition the user will be issued with a cash card. Some banks *combine* cheque cards and cash cards together now.

Each cash card holder has a maximum limit for each day or week and requests outside this limit (or if there is no money in the account) will be refused.

⇄ *Cashing a cheque*

If a cheque is being cashed then the word 'cash' is substituted for the name of the payee, as in the example below.

Note the wording that has been written *sideways* on the cheque, through the two vertical lines.

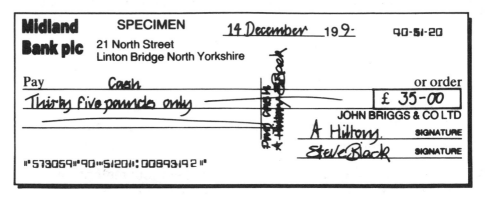

The two vertical lines printed on a cheque mean the cheque is **crossed**. A crossed cheque is safer than one which is not crossed because it *must* be paid into a bank account and cannot be cashed. Whilst this is normally better (if a cheque was lost nobody could obtain cash for it) it prevents cash being obtained. To change this situation the crossing has to be cancelled and the cheque **opened**.

This is done by writing the words *pay cash* and adding the signature of the drawer *inside* the crossing.

SPECIAL NOTE

Many banks still do not like this method as there is obviously a risk of fraud or the wrong person obtaining cash. They will prefer a cheque to be made out to the person concerned (the payee) and then the cheque 'opening' in the same way. The payee must provide evidence of identity at the bank.

Cash may be required for a till float, petty cash or to pay wages. In each case certain denominations of coins will be required – a till float of £25 is useless if it comprises 2 × £10 notes and 1 × £5 note!

CHECK IT YOURSELF
Assume you have to obtain £30 in cash as a till float. How many coins of each denomination would you choose so that you will be able to give change easily at the beginning of the day? Discuss your answer with your tutor.

FOREIGN CURRENCY

In addition to exchanging cheques for British currency, you may have to cash a cheque to buy foreign currency if someone is travelling abroad. Banks usually need prior notification of foreign currency requirements – especially if the amount required is large or the currency is one which is not often requested. Beware too, that some countries have restrictions on the amount of foreign currency which can be taken into the country.

Follow the procedures listed below when obtaining currency for foreign travel.

1   Telephone the bank and tell them your request – if possible at least 7 days before you will need the money.

2   Check there are no restrictions on the amount you are requesting.

3   You can ask the bank if you can receive the money in certain denominations, eg 6 × $50 bills not 3 = $100 bills – but you may be told that you have to accept what is sent!

4   Find out the approximate exchange rate and the bank commission so that you can given this information to your Chief Cashier, if required.

5   On the day you are collecting the money, telephone the bank first to find out the exact amount your cheque must be made out for. This will depend on the exchange rate in operation on the day the bank actually obtained the currency for you.

6   Make out the cheque for the specified amount, have it signed and take it to the bank.

7   Check that the calculations on the bank form you are given are correct in terms of the currency you have received and the amount you have paid for it.

Checking currency calculations

A bank form will have headings similar to those shown below:

Country	Currency Amount	Rate	Sterling Equivalent	Commission	Net Sterling
France	5850	9.8	596.94	1.80	598.74

CHECK IT YOURSELF

Look at the entries above and see if the bank is correct:

- the sterling equivalent is the foreign currency amount *divided by* the rate, ie $5850 \div 9.8$
- you can cross check this by *multiplying* the sterling equivalent by the rate to get the currency amount, ie 596.94×9.8
- the amount due is the sterling equivalent amount *plus* the commission – the total is given in the column Net Sterling.

SECTION REVIEW

Having completed this section, you should now be able to:

1 Explain the security measures which should be taken when taking money to the bank.

2 Correctly analyse cash and complete a bank paying-in slip including cash, cheques and postal orders.

3 Explain the common errors which may occur and how these should be rectified.

4 Pay in cash, cheques and postal orders at the bank.

5 Cash a cheque for British or foreign currency.

6 Check the amount of foreign currency against the sterling equivalent and net amount required.

REVIEW QUIZ

True or false?

1 Coins must be analysed into denominations before a paying-in slip is completed.

2 PIN stands for proper identity number.

3 Takings should be banked at the same time every day.

4 Foreign coins are not accepted by a bank.

5 To cash a cheque all you have to do is to write 'cash' instead of the payee's name.

Complete the blanks ...

6 Try to notify the bank of foreign currency requirements ......
days in advance.

7 Bags should never contain .... coins.

8 Banks prefer an 'opened' cheque to be made out to a ....
.... rather than made out for cash.

Work it out

9 Make out a bank paying-in slip, dated today, for the following:

2 cheques — Mr T Wood – £189.52, Ms C Bonham –
£532.90

2 postal orders – Mr G Sulaman – £18.60, Miss J. O'Connell –
£60.28

Cash – 3 × £50 notes   38 × £1 coins   13 × 10p coins
6 × £20 notes   11 × 50p coins   23 × 2p coins
5 × £5 notes   14 × 20p coins   2 × 1p coins

10 **a** What figures should be entered into the blank columns on the form below?
b What should be the total amount of your cheque?
c Can you find out the name of the currency for each country given below?

Country	Currency Amount	Rate	Sterling Equivalent	£ Commission	Net Sterling
Germany	1160	2.90		1.70	
France	7776	9.72		1.70	
USA	1196.92	1.84		1.70	
Belgium	31065.72	59.65		1.70	
Holland	1159.35	3.275		1.70	

Section 4 – Making payments to suppliers and others

In business most suppliers are paid by cheque:

- after any invoices have been carefully checked and passed for payment
- after the statement has been received at month end showing the total amount due for that month
- after the statement has been checked to make sure that all invoices, credit notes and payments to date have been included and calculated correctly.

INVOICES, CREDIT NOTES AND STATEMENTS

Invoices

Invoices are issued by suppliers detailing the goods which have been despatched, the price, VAT charges, any discounts and the total amount due. All invoices must be carefully checked before they are passed for payment.

If an organisation undercharges for an item a Supplementary Invoice will be sent, detailing the additional amount due.

Credit notes

Credit notes are issued when the buyer has been overcharged. This may be because of an error on the invoice or because some goods were returned to the supplier, eg because they were faulty.

Statements

At the end of the month the supplier issues a statement. This shows:

- the balance which was owing at the beginning of the month
- any invoices which have been issued during the month
- any credit notes which have been issued during the month
- any payments which have been received during the month
- the new balance.

			Number	200/689	
STATEMENT			Date	30 April 19—	

Browns of Bath
14 Crescent Parade
Bath
BT3 4PS

VAT Registration Number
209/48927/62

TO: P Robinson & Co Ltd

14 Spa Road

CHELTENHAM   CL3 9DS

Account No   3920/TM

Date	Particulars	Debit	Credit	Balance
1 April	Balance			£702.00
3 April	Invoice S27320	£200.00		£902.00
7 April	Invoice S27389	£1004.68		£1002.68
10 April	Cheque		£702.00	£300.68
14 April	Credit Note CR68		£200.00	£500.68
18 April	Invoice S 28372	£350.00		£850.68
24 April	Credit Note CR89		£62.50	£788.18
28 April	Invoice S 29378	£250.00		£1038.18
29 April	Credit Note CR95	£100.00		£938.18

■ **SPECIAL NOTE**
- The debit column shows amounts owing to the supplier.
- The credit column shows deductions from this, eg payments and credit notes.
- The balance column is completed after each transaction.

⇄ *Checking the documents*

You will probably already have had experience in checking invoices. Credit notes must be checked to make sure that the price and discounts for the goods match those on the invoice.

Statements must be checked to make sure no payment, invoice or credit note has been omitted.

All documents should be checked to make sure that the calculations are correct *before* any cheque is made out in payment.

✓ **TEST YOURSELF**
1 Why did P Robinson pay £702 on 10 April?
2 Test your checking skills! There are 4 errors in the statement above – can you find them and state the correct amount owing to Browns at the end of the month?

■ **SPECIAL NOTE**

On some accounts the buyer is offered a cash discount if he pays promptly. Unless your organisation operates a different procedure, such payments must be made whilst the option for the discount is still in force, so that the lower amount can be paid.

✓ **TEST YOURSELF**
1 Make out cheques in payment of two accounts. One for £149.65 to Midvale Office Suppliers and one for £69 to Copyrite Ltd. Date both with today's date but *do not sign them*. (If you have forgotten how to write cheques, look back at page 127.)
2 You have received an account from the local florist, who is not registered for VAT, for £25.00 less 2½% discount if the account is paid in 10 days. What is the amount due if you pay promptly?

SPECIAL NOTE
VAT is always added on after all discounts have been deducted. The current rate is 15%.

TEST YOURSELF
You have received three accounts – all of which offer discount if paid promptly. All the companies are registered for VAT. What is the amount due on each one if a) you pay immediately   b) you pay after the cash discount option has expired? (Remember the VAT figure does not change.)

1 Superware Ltd   £145.60 – 10% trade discount – 5% cash discount if paid in 10 days + VAT
2 Coleman & Green Ltd   £527.00 – 5% trade discount – 2½% cash discount if paid in 14 days + VAT
3 Cookham Travel Ltd   £228.50 – 7½% cash discount if paid in 7 days + VAT.

AUTHORISATION PROCEDURES
The authorisation procedures vary from one organisation to another and will also vary depending on the amount of the payment. Obviously there are stricter regulations governing the payment of large amounts, eg

- up to £200 one authorised signature is required on the cheque
- between £200 and £1000 two authorised signatures are required (one a director)
- £1000 to £10000 requires two directors' signatures
- above £10000 authorisation also required by the Managing Director.

Note that the above is only an example of an authorisation procedure – it is important that you check the actual procedure in force in any organisation where you are responsible for making payments.

PAYING ACCOUNTS
It is not usual to simply put a cheque in an envelope and send it off! If this was done the organisation receiving it would not know what the cheque was for without referring to its accounts.

For this reason it is usual to enclose a **remittance advice** with all cheques, stating the reason for payment.

You may find that a remittance advice is included as a tear-off form on an invoice you receive. In this case you can simply detach the form and return it with the cheque. Companies often issue invoices like this so that they can easily identify cheque payments received from private individuals.

Most business organisations, however, have their own remittance advice forms, as shown below.

```
T ROSS LTD                        REMITTANCE ADVICE

Craiglands Industrial Estate

EXETER   5EX 9PF
                                  YOUR INV    4893/SL
  ┌                    ┐
                                  INV   AMT    £423.89
   Booth & Walker Ltd
   14 Maritime Way                OUR   REF    OFF/2110
   TORQUAY
   TR4 7DM                       ┌─────────────────────────────┐
  └                    ┘         │ TOTAL VALUE OF CHEQUE  £423.89│
                                 └─────────────────────────────┘

  DATE:    19 May 199–      CREDITOR NO:  0952  CHEQUE NO 001291
```

⚠ SPECIAL NOTE

The four small marks around the name and address of the creditor denote where the address must be typed or printed so that the remittance advice can go in a window envelope with the cheque behind it. This saves the Accounts Department having to type an ordinary envelope.

Technology update

Many organisations today produce all their accounts on computer. A remittance advice would therefore be printed automatically when payment was being made. The computer can also be used to print out the cheques automatically and these can then be transferred to a cheque signing machine for automatic printing of signatures.

This system is only likely to be used in large organisations paying hundreds or thousands of cheques each month. Obviously such a machine is kept under lock and key when not in use and strictly supervised when in use.

Other types of notification

An organisation which pays out refunds on a fairly regular basis may have a standard letter printed to accompany such cheques. In this case only the variables would be completed when a refund is made. Most large holiday operators use this type of standard letter.

TEST YOURSELF

Assume you work for a large holiday booking agent. You have been asked to compose a short, standard letter to accompany any refund cheques. In addition to the basic text of the letter there should be space for:

- holiday booking reference
- amount of cheque
- passenger name(s)
- departure date
- cheque number
- reason for refund
- destination
- refund reference number.

Design and write a suitable letter and check the contents with your tutor. Then type it on a word processor and think up details to complete three letters to different clients.

Paying out cash

Cash payments may be made in certain circumstances, ie to employees reclaiming their expenses. If you are involved in making cash payments:

- ask for identification unless you know the person well
- make sure the person receiving the money signs for it
- count out the money – as a double check to both yourself and the recipient.

Don't pay money to one person on another person's behalf unless you are expressly instructed to do so by your supervisor. You must always make sure that the person who is being paid the money is the one who is authorised to receive it.

Other payments

In the same way that private individuals do not pay all their accounts by cheque, neither do businesses. In some cases they may take advantage of the wide variety of bank services available.

BANK PAYMENT SERVICES

There are a variety of bank services where money is transferred through the banking system from one account to another.

CHECK IT YOURSELF

Look at the bottom of any type of bill you or your parents receive regularly, eg gas, electricity, telephone, water rates etc. Here you will see a special printed form with the words Bank Giro Credit at the top, similar to the one shown below.

G Girobank Trans/cash	**TELECOM**	Payment Counterfoil	**Bank Giro Credit**
Girobank plc Bootle Merseyside GIR 0AA		By transfer from Girobank a/c no	

Customer account number	Credit account number	Amount due
155 205 285 2736 2036	616 9082	£ 54.18

No fee payable at PO counter
Cheque acceptable

Cashier's stamp and initials

Signature

Date

16 – 90 – 82   Cash

The Royal Bank of Scotland plc   Cheques
Head office Collection Account

LANCS & CUMBRIA   British Telecommunications plc   TOTAL £
Lancs and Cumbria District

No. of   Fee
Cheques

Please do not fold this counterfoil or mark or write below this line

```
MR  T K EDDLESTON
15 LAKESIDE DRIVE
WINDERMERE
WM3 9AQ
```

Bank giro credit

If you complete a Bank Giro Credit form and take it to the bank –
together with your cheque or cash for the amount stated – the
bank will automatically transfer the money to the account stated
on the form – on page 150 to British Telecom Account 6169082.
It doesn't matter where in the country this account is held.

Standing orders

An alternative method which bank account holders can use to
transfer money from one account to another is by **standing
order**. The standing order form instructs the bank to transfer a
fixed amount of money at regular intervals to another account. It
is used to pay mortgages, insurance premiums or subscriptions.

The form gives all the details of the payee's account, as shown in
the example below:

Direct debit

Although the standing order system saves the customer the
trouble of having to keep posting cheques to an organisation, if
the amount of money to be paid changes, or if the payments are
not made regularly then it can be inconvenient to keep having to
notify the bank of the changes.

Therefore, in cases where payments are likely to vary from one
period to another it is more usual for bank customers to use the
direct debit system.

PART TWO: INSTRUCTIONS TO YOUR BANK TO PAY DIRECT DEBITS

(Full postal address)
To: The manager _MIDLAND_ Bank
MARKET STREET
ABERDEEN Postcode

■ I instruct you to pay Direct Debits from my account at the request of
Guardian Royal Exchange Assurance plc.
■ The amounts are fixed and are to be debited on various dates.
■ I understand that Guardian Royal Exchange Assurance plc may change the
amounts and dates only after giving me prior notice.
■ I will inform the Bank in writing if I wish to cancel this Instruction.
■ I understand that if any Direct Debit is paid which breaks the terms of this
instruction, the Bank will make a refund.

Bank or Giro Account No. 3 0 4 9 8 2 6 5 0

Bank Sort Code (see top right hand corner
of your cheque book) 4 0 – 2 0 – 1 8

Name(s) of Account Holder(s)
MISS JANE HOWARTH

Note for Bank
Correspondence about this instruction should be sent to: Guardian Royal
Exchange, Life Accounts Dept, Ballam Road, Lytham St Annes, FY8 4JZ.

9 9 0 4 9 1

Signature(s)
Jane Howarth

Date _15/1/199-_

Banks may refuse to accept instructions to pay Direct Debits from some types of account

Facts about Direct Debiting
Direct Debiting is a simple, inexpensive and convenient way of paying your premium.
All you need to do is sign and return the instruction which authorises your Bank to
debit your account when your premiums are payable.
The processing of the instruction may result in some delay in collecting the first premium(s).
Such delay will never exceed three months and does not affect your rights under the policy.
The payment date(s) will be determined by GRE when your application is accepted.
The instruction has been designed so that you do not have to enter the amount of your premium.
No collection of premium will be made before it is due and the amount collected will be stated in
your policy. If GRE should request payment in error, you may seek immediate reimbursement
from GRE through your Bankers under an indemnity lodged in their favour by GRE.
You may cancel your Direct Debit Instruction at any time by notifying your Bank and GRE
accordingly.

Direct debit forms are printed by the organisation for its customers, *not* by the bank. The organisation sends this form to customers who may be interested in paying by direct debit. The customer completes it, returns it to the organisation and they then forward it to the bank.

The form authorises the customer's bank to pay the organisation from the customer's account as required.

TEST YOURSELF

1 From the details shown on the standing order form, how much will Jane Howarth pay her insurance company in total next year?

2 What advantages do you think there are in using the standing order system?

3 Can you think of any disadvantages?

4 Compare the standing order with the direct debit on page 151.

To ✸ **The Royal Bank of Scotland plc**	**Standing Order**

Please make the payments detailed below and debit my/our   Current account

Name of A/c to be debited __Jane P Howarth__   A/c No __06492100__

Reference No to be quoted __HO/TD/4831__   Date __15 Jan 199–__
(if any)

Name of Payee __Grampian Insurance co__   A/c No __42736814__

Address of Payee __Thistle Street__
                 __Edinburgh EH1 7SE__

Bank & Branch to which __National Westminster Bank__ Code No __60-01-01__
payment is to be made __Ainsle Street__
                      __Edinburgh EH3 4PT__

Amount (in words) __FIFTEEN POUNDS__
                                            £ __1500__

Date of payments __Second of each month__

Date of first payment __2 Feb 199–__

Special instructions (if any) ____

• Payments are to continue until __FURTHER NOTIFICATION__

* Payments are to continue until you receive further notice in writing
This instruction cancels any previous order in favour of the Payee named above under this reference.

Signature __Jane Howarth__

* Delete as necessary
04805 (9/84)

Security

Only recognised organisations are allowed to submit direct debit mandates to banks, eg electricity and gas boards, insurance companies and building societies etc. This prevents any 'cowboy' operators helping themselves to money from customers' accounts when they wish! The organisation *must* notify the customer if the payment details change.

TEST YOURSELF

List the advantages of using the direct debit system rather than standing order.

Credit transfer

When employees start working for an organisation they have the option of being paid in cash, by cheque or by credit transfer. If they choose credit transfer then their wages or salary will be paid direct into their bank account each week or month.

TRANSFERRING MONEY – AT HOME . . . . . .

CHAPS

CHAPS stands for Clearing House Automated Payment System and this is used by all the banks to transfer money for their clients quickly across the country. The main High Street banks are linked to CHAPS via computer and the information is merely keyed in at one branch and relayed onwards to the receiving bank by CHAPS.

. . . . . . AND ABROAD

Eurocheque

Holders of Eurocheque books can make out a Eurocheque in any currency and send this abroad to pay for goods. Note – more and more countries are joining the Eurocheque system – it is *not* just restricted to countries such as France and Spain, which are geographically situated in Europe.

Standard transfer or urgent transfer

These are computerised methods of transferring funds abroad – the urgent method costs slightly more but is quicker. The service operates to any country in the world. The customer specifies the payee, his bank and the amount to be paid. The British bank then contacts (by computer) the nearest correspondent bank abroad to where the money is to be paid. The correspondent bank then relays the money onwards.

TEST YOURSELF

From what you have read on bank payment services, which service would you recommend in each of the following cases?

1　To pay business insurance premiums to the insurance company.
2　To pay staff salaries.
3　A solicitor wishes to send his client's deposit for a house urgently across the country.
4　To pay the deposit on a hotel booking in the south of France.

SECTION REVIEW

Having completed this section, you should now be able to:

1　Check payment requests for accuracy and authorisation.

2　Identify discrepancies and errors on statements of account.

3　Explain how invoices, credit notes and payments made are calculated on the statement of account to give the balance owing.

4　Complete cheques accurately.

5　Complete remittance advice forms.

6　Describe the circumstances under which payment must be made promptly.

7　Calculate discounts and VAT.

8　List the procedure to follow when paying out cash.

9　State the main bank payment services and why they are used.

10　Explain how authorisation procedures may differ between small and large payments

True or false?

1 Cash discounts are offered to encourage prompt payment.

2 Credit notes are issued when the buyer has been overcharged.

3 Statements are issued at the beginning of each month.

4 Eurocheques can only be used for countries situated within Europe.

5 A direct debit can only be used to pay a fixed sum of money at regular intervals.

Complete the blanks ...

6 A person claiming a cash payment should be asked for
....

7 The form which is sent to accompany cheques in payment is called a ....

8 Completed direct debit forms are sent to the ....

Work it out

9 You have received a statement from Daniel & Sons, of Wolverhampton. According to your records the balance at the start of the month is correct. This month:

- you have paid them 3 cheques for £132, £300.20 and £42.18.

- you have received goods on 3 occasions. The invoice details are as follows:

    Invoice S 58279 £223.59 – 10% trade discount + VAT

    Invoice S 62892 £816.42 – 10% trade discount + VAT

    Invoice S 70982 £230.80 – 10% trade discount + VAT (this was a special order subject to 2½ discount if you pay it within 14 days)